MW00570619

How to Succeed
in Business
as an
Executive
Assistant

How to Succeed in Business as an Executive Assistant

By Melba J. Duncan

with Kathleen Moloney

Collier Books
Macmillan Publishing Company
New York
Collier Macmillan Publishers
London

Copyright © 1989 by Melba J. Duncan and Kathleen Moloney

"Proofreading test" reprinted courtesy of Law Publications, Los Angeles

"In Basket test" reprinted courtesy of Karen R. Gillespie,
New York University

All rights reserved. No part of this book may be reproduced or transmitted
in any form or by any means, electronic or mechanical, including
photocopying, recording, or by any information storage and retrieval system,
without permission in writing from the Publisher.

Collier Books
Macmillan Publishing Company
866 Third Avenue, New York, NY 10022
Collier Macmillan Canada, Inc.

Library of Congress Cataloging-in-Publication Data
Duncan, Melba J.
How to succeed in business as an executive assistant/by Melba J.
Duncan with Kathleen Moloney.
p.   cm.
Includes index.
ISBN 0-02-031790-5
1. Office practice—Vocational guidance. 2. Corporation
secretaries—Vocational guidance. I. Moloney, Kathleen.
II. Title.
HF5547.5.D84   1989
658.4—dc20   89-7053   CIP

Macmillan books are available at special discounts for bulk purchases
for sales promotions, premiums, fund-raising, or educational use.
For details, contact:

Special Sales Director
Macmillan Publishing Company
866 Third Avenue
New York, NY 10022

Design by Ellen R. Sasahara

10 9 8 7 6 5 4 3 2 1

Printed in the United States of America

Contents

Contents

Contents

Acknowledgments

IF IT WEREN'T for the Duncan Group, I would never have thought about writing this book, so it seems only right to take this opportunity to thank the two people who helped me get the business started. For their advice, their enthusiasm, and their support I am grateful to Peter G. Peterson and Russell S. Reynolds, Jr. I must also give my heatfelt thanks to Zalman C. Bernstein, without whom I would never have acquired the skills and courage to pursue this career.

I'm also most grateful to the people who help me keep the business running smoothly, especially my associate, Barbara Werber, who was often "counterpoint" to my "point" as we worked with the writer on the book, and my executive assistant, Pat Reagan.

For their opinions, insights, and war stories I thank Barbara Bennett, Debbie Brown, Roberta Corcoran, Daniel Doolin, Joyce Gibson, Judith Ann Gustafson, Susan Lehman, Carol Morrow, Elva Murphy, Barbara Neysmith, Karen Richards, Carolyn Seergy, and Mary Ann Watts.

For their advice and editorial help I thank my agent, Dominick Abel, and my editors, John Glusman and Robert Kimzey.

My final thanks go to my husband, Max, and my daughter, Michelle, for everything.

Author's Note

The material in this book is based on my own experiences (before I started the Duncan Group, I worked for twenty years as an executive assistant) and those of more than a dozen willing reporters who are currently holding down the job. The companies they work for are large, medium-sized, and small, profit and non-. A few have been doing the job for as long as twenty-five years, and some are just starting out. They're all smart, hard-working, and opinionated about the role of executive assistant in general and their work in particular. They shared their experiences, speaking very candidly, with the assurance that I would not use their names or otherwise identify my sources in the book. That's why I attribute the many quotes and stories herein to "an executive assistant I know" instead of giving you the person's name, rank, and serial number. I hope this will not prove to be too disconcerting.

Another thing I've done is refer to executive assistants as "her" and "she" and executives as "him" and "he." I had two reasons: one, it would have been awkward to go the "he or she" or "that person" route; and two, that's pretty much the way it is. The Department of Commerce says that the number of male secretaries is climbing steadily; it's up to about seventy-five thousand, which is a 24 percent increase since 1972. Still, that number represents less than 2 percent of the secretarial force. Others estimate the percentage of male secretaries at about 10. I don't know the percentage of executives who are male, but I'm sure it's well over 50 percent. In the absence of an all-purpose pronoun, I chose the ones that made the most sense.

Introduction

Have I Got a Job for You!

IN the summer of 1985, when the Duncan Group first opened its doors for business, I was invited to talk about my new venture on the "Today Show." Appearing with me were the other members of the Duncan Group board, Russell S. Reynolds, Jr., chairman of Russell Reynolds Associates, and Peter G. Peterson, chairman of the Blackstone Group.

When Bryant Gumbel asked Mr. Peterson why he, a busy and important executive, was taking an interest in a fledgling organization that specializes in recruiting administrative assistants and executive secretaries, his answer spoke volumes. "Rarely do my head and my heart and my pocketbook all end up at the same place," he said. He went on to explain that his heart was with me because we had worked together so long and so well (I was his assistant for ten years when he was chairman of Lehman Brothers Kuhn Loeb); his head told him that because the most important person in every executive's business life is a really good assistant, there was a real need for my service; and his pocketbook anticipated a high return on his investment.

I tell this story not to boast about the Duncan Group but by

1

way of introduction to my favorite subject—the extraordinary opportunities available to the executive assistant. I myself did the job for twenty years, and I loved just about every minute of it. Today my work involves putting the right assistant together with the right executive, and in doing so I can spread a little of my enthusiasm around. With this book I hope to spread my enthusiasm and expertise still further.

The plain and simple fact is that, for any number of reasons, many smart, eminently qualified women are simply not making it in management today. According to the U.S. Department of Labor, women hold the majority of professional jobs in the country, yet according to the most recent statistics, women earn considerably less than men in the Professional category—$419 a week, compared to $581. In July of 1987 the *New York Times* reported that women receive 68 percent of the average wage earned by men.

In short, times are tough for women who want top jobs, and unfulfilled expectations abound among the women in middle management. Here many of them are, a few years out of college, earning $18,000 to $22,500 a year as junior executives, and they have to face the fact that this may be as good as it gets. What's more, the barriers that some women face are not measured just in dollars and cents. In trying to compete in the same arenas with men they may come up against psychological, physical, and chauvinistic barriers, all of which can detract from the satisfaction of doing a job.

It's my belief that for many women the solution to this "middle management is a dead end" problem is to become an executive assistant—sometimes called an "administrative assistant" or "executive secretary." Women in high-level secretarial positions don't have to compete with anyone, and many of their jobs are far more interesting, challenging, and powerful than the middle management positions they used to fill. They may also pay a lot better; we regularly place people at anything from $25,000 to $70,000, depending on education, experience, and the demands of the position.

I don't kid myself. I realize all too well that there continues to be a stigma attached to being "just a secretary" and that the stereotype puts some people off. I see it as a vicious circle. Because of its less than stellar reputation, the secretarial field has often attracted people with less than stellar skills, who can't speak properly or spell or use the phone efficiently. However, as better educated, more experienced people are made aware of the opportunities and enter the field, the myth of the gum-chewing, nail-filing *Nine to Five* secretary will eventually be put to rest. In this book I've offered specific advice about how to perform every aspect of the executive assistant's job well, in the hope that my efforts will serve to elevate the reputation of the position still more.

I know too that executive assistant jobs are not right for everyone. The hours are hard, the stress can be rough, you have to deal with difficult personalities, and job security is a real problem. But if you're a person who has a sound education and excellent secretarial skills, who does not need to be in the limelight, who enjoys being a support person, who likes communicating with people and solving problems, who has judgment, tact, and discretion, have I got a job for you!

I've had a good time writing *How to Succeed in Business as an Executive Assistant.* It has brought back a lot of memories and given me a chance to think about and refine my thoughts about how to get a good job in this business and how to do it well once you have it. I hope that after reading it you'll be inspired to give this line of work a try.

PART I

How to Succeed in Business as an Executive Assistant

IN my introduction I gave what I think of as my Knute Rockne speech, talking about the wonders that await the person who chooses a career as an executive assistant. Here in part 1, I get a little more specific. In these four chapters I cover the benefits and drawbacks of the job, the qualifications you need to get the job, how to land the job, and the unique relationship between an executive assistant and her boss.

1

The Job Description

ONE executive assistant I know works for the president of a huge Fortune 500 company. The executive she reports to has four children, two homes, and a wife who runs her own small business. He travels about two weeks out of every four, entertains often, and routinely puts in a ten-hour day. It takes a support staff of five to keep his affairs in order: a senior secretary, a number-two secretary, a word processor, a clerk, and my friend the executive assistant, who keeps it all running smoothly. When I asked her to give me her job description, she didn't miss a beat. "Whatever it takes," she said. "If I had to write a résumé, I'd be in trouble."

What my friend said is true of virtually every executive assistant. When you work for an executive, you do, quite simply, what needs to be done. That means you type, file, meet and greet visitors to the office, read and organize the mail, take dictation, transcribe notes, compose letters, make travel arrangements, answer the phone and place calls, make his appointments, and keep his calendar. You may also order supplies, prepare budgets, pay bills, and run what one assistant I know refers to as a twenty-four-hour beverage service.

I did all that and a lot more during my years as an executive assistant, and if I said I loved every minute of it, I wouldn't be telling the truth. As any executive assistant will tell you, there is good news and bad news about this job.

The Best Parts of the Job

The perks of the job can be substantial; most of the assistants I spoke to mentioned good salaries, bonuses, gifts, and travel. One person described a job that gave her access to a car and driver. But when asked what they liked best about the job, most executive assistants concentrated on the less tangible pleasures and satisfactions of their jobs.

You Get to Be Near Power

"A few months ago I worked very hard to put together a big sales presentation for my boss," an assistant told me. "The morning after he gave the presentation, there was a story about it in the business section of the paper. Then, a couple of weeks later, my boss was quoted on the front page. That kind of thing makes me feel important."

That kind of thing makes virtually *everyone* feel important. There's something very exhilarating about working in an environment in which significant decisions are being made. When you work closely for someone at the top or close to it, you can't help but be swept along.

You're Never Bored

Perhaps I should say you're *almost* never bored. I've never met anyone who wasn't bored senseless by filing. Even so, the average assistant's job has enough variety to keep you stimulated. "To me the best part of the job is that no two days are alike," an assistant said. "When my boss's phone rings, the person on the other end could want to talk to me about any of a dozen different things."

Another assistant told me about her brief retirement from the life of executive assistant. After a few years of working for a senior vice-president she was promoted to manager of secretarial services. "I know that it was supposed to be a step up—after all, it was officially middle management—but the truth is, I was bored to death. Every day was pretty much the same. I lasted a year and then got a job as assistant to the president."

You Get to Be Independent

In doing "whatever it takes" to do this job well an executive assistant doesn't just type and file and follow orders. She also runs interference, makes decisions, and protects her boss from the outside world. Rising to the challenge of decision making is one of the most gratifying aspects of this job. As one person told me, "I love carving out an area that I'm in charge of completely. It makes me happy that I've won my boss's trust enough so that he lets me speak for him."

You Always Know What's Going On

As I'll discuss in chapter 4, you aren't allowed to gossip on this job, but you are allowed to know a great deal, perhaps more than even the boss himself, about what's going on in your organization. In fact, you can't help but be aware of every little organizational tremor, with the confidential reports and other documents that pass through your IN box. "I get a real charge out of the fact that I have access to information that even the vice-presidents don't always have," one assistant said. She is not alone.

You Meet Interesting People

"I talked to an actress, a U.S. senator, and several millionaires before lunch this morning," one assistant told me. "Everyone I talk to on the phone is at the top of his field," said another. Rich, famous, powerful, and influential people aren't always interesting, of course, but they are often enough. You won't be bored.

You Get Respect

None of the executive assistants I know kids herself about being powerful (or even popular) in her own right. Each realizes all too well that any prestige she enjoys comes to her because of her boss's position, not her own. Still, being treated with respect is pleasant no matter what the reason. "Because I work for the chairman, people are polite, almost deferential, to me," one assistant said. "Some of them go overboard, being extra nice in the hopes that I'll put in a good word for them with the boss. I don't mind it a bit."

You Get an Education

I suppose it's possible to do this job without learning anything, but you'd have to try awfully hard. Most people find the work enormously educational if they have the right boss. "After working for him for ten years I feel as if I've gotten a degree in business," one assistant said. "I've learned not just about this business but also about how to *do* business." In my twenty years of watching my bosses plan, hire and fire, direct and motivate a staff, and create a productive work environment, I learned enough to run my own business.

You Can Make a Difference

Most of the people who choose this job and who succeed at it have a need to be needed and get enormous satisfaction out of helping others. Working for an executive satisfies that desire to make a real difference. One assistant summed it up for all of those I spoke to when she said, "I know I can't be chairman of the board. I'm not even sure I'd *want* to be if I got the chance. But I can run the chairman's office, and once in a while I can put my two cents in. Knowing that I make things better really makes me happy."

The Worst Parts of the Job

Being an executive assistant can be great, but it's not perfect. It can try your patience, play havoc with your social life, and if you gobble enough ten-minute lunches, wreck your digestion. Here are the most common complaints I've heard.

You Work Long Hours

As far as I can tell, there's no such thing as a nine-to-five executive assistant job. Ten- to twelve-hour days are more common. The more highly placed your boss is, the worse it gets. One busy assistant said, "Sometimes I dream about taking the afternoon off and going to a museum, but it's just not in the cards. I can't even keep a dentist appointment."

You Can Get Pigeonholed

As a "support person" you may feel stifled and frustrated, particularly when you know you are capable of much more than you're doing or feel that your contributions are not sufficiently recognized and appreciated. It's hard to advance unless you have a boss who gives you a chance to grow in the job.

You Have to Keep a Low Profile

The boss can be moody and temperamental, talk nonstop about his life and tell you his troubles, and cover his office walls with cute pictures of his family, his pets, and his sailboat if he wants to. As his assistant you can't do any of the above. If you're having a crisis at home or you're in a bad mood, you have to leave it

11

outside and pretend that everything is fine. I heard a story about an assistant who made the mistake of confiding in her boss when she was going through a divorce. A few months later her boss used the information against her when he fired her. "Look, I know that you're having a rough time these days, but I can't help that," he said. "I need someone who is paying full attention."

Unlike the boss, you can't treat your office as a home away from home. He can turn his space into a miniature golf course, but yours has to look professional. A couple of small, discreet photographs are acceptable, but anything else is out of place. Some assistants resent not being able to treat their offices as home. "After all," they say, "if the boss has a pool table in his office, why can't I have my dart board and a few mementos? I'm a person too." The sentiment is understandable but unrealistic. The unvarnished truth is that the office you work in is *his* office, not yours.

Age Can Be a Problem

To a great many executives the ideal assistant is a twenty-five-year-old woman with twenty years of experience. It's illegal for employers to discriminate on the basis of age, but to be honest, a woman over forty-five may have a problem finding work in this field, and a woman over fifty-five is very difficult to place. (Of course, that's true in almost every field.) Fortunately, for those few employers who think that someone over forty-five is also over the hill, there's one who appreciates the experience and judgment, not to mention the Rolodex, that come with age.

We welcome the challenge of placing women of "a certain age," provided they have the energy, enthusiasm, and openmindedness usually associated with younger people. If you stay active and continue to be open to new ways of doing things, you'll do fine.

It's Stressful

There are several aspects of this job that make a strong woman gnash her teeth once in a while, but one gets exceptionally high ratings on the Stress Meter: You never have the luxury of working on one project until it's finished. ("In this job you're always reacting to something, always having to stop in midjob to solve a problem or put out a fire," one assistant said.) Having to juggle at least two things at once all the time can be hard on people with a passion for order.

Job Security Is Shaky

When your boss leaves the company—because he retires or takes another job or gets ousted or decides to give it all up and sail around the world—normally that means you have to pack up your things and leave as well. For better or for worse, you are considered an appendage to the executive for whom you work. This can have its advantages, of course, but it can also be a real problem, especially when the boss gets a "golden parachute," but you get one that won't even open. "I worked for an executive for ten years," one assistant said. "When he was ousted in a power play, he got six-figure severance. I had to prove that they owed me vacation pay." Protecting yourself by negotiating a good benefits package can alleviate this problem (see chapter 3), but unfortunately nothing will make it go away.

You Have to Make Coffee

Every executive assistant job description comes with tasks that could be considered above and beyond the call of duty. Everyone does them, but I've never met a soul who was very happy about it. There is much more about this subject in chapter 4.

Opportunities

According to the Bureau of Labor Statistics, between 1986 and the year 2000 there will be a a 13.1 percent increase in the number of secretarial jobs in this country. The agency projects that there will be 475,000 new secretarial openings annually through 1995. What's more, it's a seller's market at the moment, since there aren't nearly enough qualified people to fill those jobs. Executives in all industries are desperate for qualified assistants right now, and the shortage is going to get worse before it gets better.

The way I see it, there is plenty of opportunity here.

Salary

The subject of salary could have been put, quite properly, under both "The Best Parts of the Job" and "The Worst Parts of the Job." Instead I decided to give it a section all its own.

Talking about salaries in any field is a dicey business at best; compensation is bound to vary tremendously from place to place, depending on many factors, including the laws of supply and demand. To confuse matters even more, the executive assistant field is very much in flux today. In some companies secretaries are regarded as typing and filing machines, virtually interchangeable; in others they're looked upon as individuals who make a special contribution. Naturally each group is paid accordingly.

Still, I'll go out on a limb and say that in New York, Boston, and Washington, D.C., a college graduate with a few years of experience and excellent clerical skills can expect to earn from $28,000 to $35,000 a year as an executive assistant. A more experienced person can easily earn as much as $50,000. We've placed someone at $70,000 a year. Someone with only a couple of years of college can expect to shave off a few thousand dollars from each category.

There are other tangible benefits of this job as well. Our candidates have asked for and received everything from bonuses, profit sharing, IRAs, special health insurance, and state-of-the-art office equipment to free tuition, an allowance for professional books and magazines, and free lunches in the company dining room.

Advancement

"I know that a lot of people see this job as a stepping-stone. They think that being someone's secretary or assistant is a good way to get started in the business. Not me. I see what I do as a *career.* The way I look at it is, I have a career working for executives."

Not everyone looks at this line of work in that way, of course. Magazines and newspapers are filled with stories of former secretaries who made it big in other fields, such as Barbara Walters, Gloria Steinem, and Helen Gurley Brown. Before she started Mary Kay Cosmetics, Mary Kay Ash was a secretary. In many fields, especially advertising, marketing, public relations, sales, fashion, and communications, women routinely sign on as secretaries or assistants in the hope of eventually making a move into management. Sometimes this works (more often in small, entrepreneurial firms than in huge companies and almost never in law, accounting, finance, and education), and sometimes it doesn't.

On the other hand, there are many opportunities for advancement for those who, like the woman I quoted above, want to carve out a career as an executive assistant. The skills you bring to one job are eminently transferable to another. Every smart, ambitious assistant I know could move happily and comfortably from company to company, industry to industry, and state to state. As one woman said, "I think what I love most about doing this for a living is knowing that I can go anywhere and find a job. Lots of people who specialize are caught up in the fear of losing their jobs. I have the kind of general job that people will always need."

Titles

Some call them *executive secretaries.* Others prefer the title *administrative assistant.* Many people will tell you that job titles don't matter, that the only thing that counts is what you do and how well you do it. I don't agree. To me the different titles mean very different things, and I think those differences matter very much, both to people in your own company and, especially, to those outside. Ask anyone for an honest opinion, and I'm sure you'll be told that *assistant* carries more clout than *secretary*. "Assistant to the president" and "assistant to the chairman" are most impressive of all.

As you can tell, the title I like most for someone who works for an executive is *executive assistant.* To me that title says, "I do many things besides type, file, and answer the phone. What's more, I work for someone important, an executive." It's not just a question of semantics; it's a matter of defining your terms. One assistant I know puts it this way: "A secretary answers the phone and takes a message. An assistant handles the call."

Before you accept a job, make sure you understand what the title is. If you think that what they're planning to call you doesn't accurately reflect what you'll be doing, try having it upgraded. This can be a problem in large, very bureaucratic companies— where they'd give people numbers instead of titles if they thought they could get away with it—but most small firms are more flexible. It doesn't hurt to give it a try.

Now that you know what the job is called, turn to the next chapter and see if you have what it takes to do it.

2

What It Takes
to Do the Job

ONE career executive assistant I know, a woman who has enjoyed considerable success, says that she owes it all to her grandmother, a sweet little old lady who demanded perfection in all things. She wanted her granddaughter to be smart, well mannered, beautifully spoken, and, of course, perfectly groomed. She trained her to exercise good judgment and tact. She encouraged her to be resourceful and, above all, to use her common sense. It's almost as if she knew her granddaughter was going to work for a CEO when she grew up.

To be an executive assistant you need not meet every demand made by my friend's grandmother, but there are educational and technical requirements that must be met. There are also certain personality traits that make you suitable for the job. What follows is a brief explanation of each.

Education

A high-school education is a prerequisite for anyone looking for a job as a secretary, but if you want to carve out a career as an

17

executive assistant, you will almost certainly need more. Even a year or two of college can make a huge difference in the job opportunities that are available to you, not to mention the salary you can command. With a college degree you can virtually write your own ticket, provided your secretarial skills are first-rate.

You don't need an Ivy League education. Community colleges that offer a degree in occupational studies are excellent, especially if you sign on for two years. Most one-year programs concentrate exclusively on essential business courses, such as typing, short-hand, word processing, and bookkeeping. In the two-year programs you get all that and a smattering of liberal arts courses as well, such as humanities, history, economics, psychology, and the social sciences.

Though you may be tempted to stick to business, I encourage you to branch out a little, if only for the most practical of reasons. The more extensive and more well-rounded your educational background is, the higher your perceived value as an employee will be. A year or two of college can mean several thousand extra dollars a year in salary.

Secretarial School

Secretarial schools have changed a lot over the last twenty years. For one thing, students no longer wear white gloves, walk with books on their heads, and take classes in how to pour tea. For another, they've become more progressive in their curriculums. These days, in addition to the standard business courses, they are likely to offer classes in psychology, speech, and human relations. One school offers a course called Organization and Management.

These are all steps in the right direction, I believe, and in general I'm very much in favor of secretarial school. It's hard not to be when I hear the graduates' success stories, like the one about the young woman who graduated from secretarial school on Friday and reported for work the following Monday as one of four secretaries working for the U.S. Attorney General. Three years later, still in her early twenties, she's one of two assistants reporting to the CEO of a large private company.

For these and other reasons many career assistants I know sing the praises of secretarial school, but several of them mentioned that the student body is likely to be a mixed bag. For every student who is there to perfect the skills that will start her out on a new career, there is one who just wants to learn how to type well enough to get by. It's not just the degree that allows you to get ahead in this field; you need ambition and drive, too. Keep in mind that the young graduate I just described graduated first in her class.

Certification

Fewer than twenty-five thousand of the four-million-plus secretaries in this country are CPSs—Certified Professional Secretaries. When a secretary is certified, she has a document, issued by the Institute of Certifying Secretaries, that proves she has taken courses in business law, economics, management, accounting, office administration, communications, and office technology and that she has passed a test on each subject.

Being certified can't hurt, and it may help. According to some sources, a certified secretary will earn one or two thousand dollars a year more than a noncertified secretary. If you're interested in knowing more about certification, write or call Professional Secretaries International at 301 E. Armour Blvd., Kansas City, MO 64111-1299, (816) 531-7010.

Technical Skills

I've discussed education before technical skills because I believe so fiercely in the value of higher education in this field, but of course, it is technical skills that are of prime importance. To put it bluntly, you can get a job as a secretary if you've never heard of Shakespeare, but no one is going to hire you if you can't type. Naturally, every executive assistant job is different, with varying technical requirements, but virtually everyone must have some expertise in the following areas.

Typing/Word Processing

In the old days, the best typists burned up the keys at one hundred words a minute, but today many people are satisfied with 50 wpm and positively thrilled with 70 to 80 wpm. Of course, the typewriter is all but extinct in today's offices, replaced by word processors and other computers. You will be expected to be as proficient on the word processor as you are on the typewriter. To complete the picture, the all-star assistant in today's world needs to know the rudiments of computer language.

Steno/Transcription

In high schools and some secretarial schools they're saying that stenography is dead. They tell you that nobody dictates to people any more, now that they have tape recorders. Some high schools and secretarial schools have even stopped teaching steno.

The trouble is, they're wrong. While it's true that a knowledge of steno is not necessary in most entry-level secretarial positions, it's also true that if you work for an executive, you'd be lost without it. Every high-level executive assistant job I've ever heard of requires knowledge of stenography. (One executive assistant at a very high level has spent twenty years working her way up the secretarial ladder. After she had two or three rungs behind her, the company sent her off to night school to learn steno.)

Still, it's true that almost everyone has realized the value of using a tape recorder. The luxury of being able to dictate and transcribe letters when only one of you is in the room has all but revolutionized office dynamics. In addition to taking steno (at about 100 wpm) you should know how to use a dictating machine and transcriber.

Accounting

Don't let the word *accounting* scare you. You don't have to be a CPA to be a good, even a first-rate, executive assistant. However, you do need an understanding of cash flow, and you should be sufficiently comfortable with numbers to be able to pay bills, work within a budget, keep financial records, balance a checkbook, calculate interest, and prepare your boss's expense account. Even if you hate math, I suggest you bite the bullet and learn a few rudimentary accounting techniques.

Communications Skills

Perhaps the most important aspect of any executive assistant's job is her ability to communicate clearly, intelligently, and pleasantly, both orally and in writing.

Writing

No matter where your formal education ends—with high school, secretarial school, or college—you must end up knowing something about spelling and grammar, and you should have a better-than-decent vocabulary. (Later I describe the tests we give for these skills.) Many assistants are required to draft letters and other documents for their bosses, and even if that doesn't happen very often, tape transcription goes a lot more smoothly when you know how to spell the words you hear and you're familiar with the rules of punctuation.

If it's been a long time since you diagrammed a sentence and your language arts skills are a little rusty, take a refresher course in English composition or curl up with a good book, such as Fowler's *Modern English Usage* or Strunk and White's *Elements of Style.* A mastery of grammar and syntax will serve you well in all that you do.

21

Speaking

One morning not too long ago a young woman came to my office to talk about the possibility of our placing her as an executive assistant. I was optimistic about her chances. Her résumé was terrific: she had worked for several middle-level executives, and on paper she appeared to be ready to move up. When she arrived, I could see that she made a nice appearance, and according to the tests we gave her before the interview, her skills were impeccable, and she was very bright. Then she started to talk, and the bubble burst. Her voice was grating, and her grammar was substandard. I had no choice but to turn her away.

In order to work for a top executive, you have to speak properly—it's as simple as that. Dropped *G*s (as in "goin'," "walkin'," and "drinkin',"), dropped *R*s (as in "drinkin' beah"), and extra *R*s (such as when you have an "idear") won't do in an executive office. Neither will a squeaky voice, a deep drawl, a tendency to rely on such rhetorical fillers as "like," "you know," and "uh," and dentalizing (hitting your *T*s and *D*s too hard, as many New Yorkers do). In fact, anything that makes you sound less than strictly professional is going to hurt your chances of getting ahead.

I'm not saying that everyone has to sound like a newscaster on the ten o'clock news; our voices give us character and make us distinctive and interesting. I *am* saying that you should know what newscasters know: The way we sound makes an enormous impression on people.

If you're not sure how your voice comes across, take a little time and try to listen to yourself when you talk on the phone or have conversations with your family, friends, and co-workers. Get a tape recorder and, using your natural voice—tone, speed, volume, the works—talk into it for at least five minutes. Play it back and listen, really listen, to your voice, identifying anything that doesn't sound correct or pleasing. This is not as easy as it seems, since an untrained ear often doesn't detect even egregious speech errors. (A speech therapist once told me that many people who say, "Wick" when they mean "Rick" can't hear the difference when you play it back to them.) Here's what you should be listening for.

Voice quality. Your voice should have a timbre that's pleasing to the ear—moderately resonant and not too loud or too soft. Women's voices can tend to be squeaky, wispy, or excessively nasal, but those are all habits that can be broken with practice. We can't all sound like Rosalind Russell or Kathleen Turner, but no one has to come across like Minnie Mouse.

Accent. Some people feel a British accent is ideal, but I have no real preferences, providing you do whatever is necessary to rid your speech of strong accents and pronounced regionalisms. Very mild accents are all right, but anything more distracts from the substance of what you're saying.

Speed. There are two things wrong with talking too fast: one, you may give the impression that you think what you have to say is so unimportant, you have to get it over with as quickly as possible; and two, you may make it hard for people to follow you. On the other hand, if you talk too slowly, people may think you're not too bright. Aim for something in the middle.

Bad speech habits. Look for those problems I mentioned above—dentalization and so on—and other annoying habits, such as slurring your words or ending declarative sentences as if they were followed by question marks.

If your attempts at self-evaluation don't pan out, you may find it helpful to ask someone whose opinion you value to give you a critique of your speaking style. However, you may not feel comfortable putting a friend on the spot like that, in which case making an appointment with a speech therapist or taking a speech class probably makes more sense. Even one session can be most beneficial; sometimes all it takes to solve a speech problem is the knowledge that you have one.

Once you've identified what you need to correct, you can embark on self-improvement. There are any number of ways to improve your speech. First, you can emulate someone who speaks well. For example, you can listen to the radio and mimic the voices you especially like to hear. Second, you can work privately with a speech therapist. One-on-one sessions can be extremely enlightening. And third, you can sign up for a course in public speaking, which will help you in at least two ways: You'll learn not just how to speak better but how to become more relaxed and comfortable while you do it.

Friendly Persuasion

An important aspect of communicating with people is the ability to put them at their ease, to make them comfortable even if you're turning down a request for an interview or making them cool their heels in the outer office for an hour. Anyone can tell someone to do something; it takes real skill (not to mention tact, diplomacy, patience, humor, and the charm of a talk-show host) to make the person like it.

In the old days there were charm schools and finishing schools for this sort of thing, but today we're on our own. You can learn some of what you need to know from books on etiquette and psychology, but I think the best way to learn how to behave graciously is to find a role model. Workplaces are brimming over with women who are the epitome of grace and charm. Find one of them and copy her.

Appearance

I realize that the rules of business attire have loosened up quite a bit over the years, but I continue (sometimes to the chagrin of those who work for me) to take a hard line when it comes to the executive assistant's dress code. I feel that if you are going to represent an executive, you have to look the part, and that involves looking professional from head to toe. In the list that follows I've explained what that means to me. If, as you read the items, you think I sound like a fuddy-duddy, remember that one of my goals here is to upgrade the image of secretaries. I'm determined to do everything in my power to dispel the stereotype of that *Nine to Five* secretary who wears tight sweaters and chews gum. Whether you like it or not, the way we look transmits a message to others. I want your appearance to say, loud and clear, "I am a professional, a serious person doing serious work." The following tips should get you started.

Consider your environment. Different businesses have different dress requirements. For instance, people in the "creative" industries, such as advertising and the media, tend to dress with a bit more flash than those in law firms and investment banking. Don't be a trendsetter. Take your cues from your co-workers.

Be conservative. Regardless of how others in your workplace are outfitted, your position as assistant to an executive dictates that you have to dress in a way that is guaranteed not to offend anyone. After all, you have to meet and greet the outside world and represent the boss, and you can't very well do that in jeans and sneakers or sandals and a low-cut dress. I'm sure that many people would give me an argument about this, but I'm against pants in the office, and I'm opposed to bare legs, even in the heat of summer.

Don't try to look like a man. Wear a gray flannel suit or a blue blazer if that's what you like, but don't feel obligated to look like one of the guys. Looking professional and at the same time fashionable and "feminine" is easier today than it used to be. Now there are lovely suits, jackets, and geared-for-business dresses in bright, warm colors and interesting fabrics.

Don't be conspicuous. If you want to look glamorous, try modeling. Support staff is not supposed to attract attention, so save the miniskirts, patterned stockings, spike heels, boots, transparent blouses, and wild jewelry for after hours. A thoroughly modern hairstyle and even colorful fingernails are fine in all but the most conservative surroundings, but a punk hairdo and black nail polish aren't right anywhere.

Design your own "uniform." Dressing for success can be an expensive proposition, it's true, but one way to get around the problem is to stick to a kind of uniform. You don't have to have a dozen different outfits; all you need is a couple of skirts, a couple of blazers, and a few blouses. I see nothing wrong in wearing a black skirt, a beautiful white blouse, and a well-cut blazer every day of the week.

Always be impeccably groomed. Even if you can't be a fashion plate every day, you can be tidy and neat, with clean, crisply pressed clothes, skin that is well cared for, and well-tended hair and fingernails. Almost every woman can benefit from a little makeup, but don't overdo it.

Look for a role model. Some people say that you should dress not for the job you're in now but for the job you want. I say look around and ask yourself, "Whom do I want to emulate?" Find someone whose appearance you admire and start trying to look like her.

Watch your posture. You can be wearing the most expensive, most beautifully tailored suit in the world, but if you slouch when you walk or slump in your chair, you look terrible. The way you carry yourself says a lot about how you regard yourself and expect to be treated by others.

Temperament

Even if you speak beautifully, look fantastic, and can type faster than a speeding bullet, you aren't necessarily cut out for this line of work. You've also got to be temperamentally suited for the job. Here are the personality traits that make a top executive assistant.

You have to have a healthy ego. To do this job well you need a strange blend of humility and confidence. If your ego is too weak, you probably won't be able to handle the responsibilities that come with working for someone in the seat of power. (Don't kid yourself—sometimes it takes nerves of steel to do this job.) If your ego is excessively inflated, there is a good chance you'll resent being out of the limelight and consider the less lofty tasks you have to perform beneath your dignity. An assistant with an ego that's somewhere between the two can do all parts of the job well without feeling like a servant.

You have to enjoy serving. "I get a real kick out of knowing that someone smart and accomplished and powerful depends on me," one assistant told me. "I've always gotten pleasure out of helping people," said another. "I work for a wonderful man who is doing valuable work. It's an honor to help him," said a third. These comments may seem a little excessive, but they're real, and they point up an important fact: Most people who do the job of executive assistant well have a genuine desire to help others. They're not saints, mind you—they'd much rather help him write the most important speech of his career than order flowers for his wife—but they do like to help others.

You have to be cool in a crisis. If you have in mind being a prima donna, you're in the wrong line of work. No matter what terrible thing happens in the course of a day, you can't let it bother you,

27

at least not so that anyone can tell. Others can have temper tantrums and crying jags; you have to stay in control.

You have to have a sense of perspective. One of the ways to keep your cool is to take the long view, to look beyond the difficult personalities or outrages of the moment and keep your eye on your ultimate goal.

You have to know how to manage stress. No matter how cool you stay in a crisis and how excellent your sense of perspective is, this job can be extraordinarily stressful. If you don't believe me, ask the average assistant how her neck feels at the end of a workday. Since you can't let off steam in the office, you need to find another way to cope with the tensions of the day. I'm a strong believer in the value of exercise as a stress reliever (I run my stress away), but I know that others are equally enthusiastic about the restorative value of deep breathing, meditation, yoga, and reading a good book. Find something that helps you "let go"; you're going to need it.

Organizational Skills

If I had to name the one overall skill that I consider more valuable than all others for an executive assistant, I'd have to say that it's the ability to manage your time. I don't like the word "prioritizing" very much, but I do like the concept.

As I said in chapter 1, one of the drawbacks of this job is that you rarely get a chance to work on one project, uninterrupted, until it's done. There's always a phone to answer, a message to pass along to your boss, or some sort of fire to put out. You're always putting someone or something on hold. What this means is that you have to know, almost instinctively, the order of importance of all the various tasks that must be accomplished and how long it will take to get them done. You need a good calendar, a great follow-up system, and the discipline it takes not to waste time.

Many executives, especially CEOs and chairmen of the board, are up to their necks in outside activities: boards, foundations, charity work, and other extracurricular interests that require the attention of an assistant. (One assistant I know who works for a chairman says she spend about half her time working on actual company matters; the rest of the time she deals with the boss's charities and the boards he sits on.) To be a good assistant to that kind of busy executive involves the kind of juggling that would put a circus performer to shame. If you're the type who can't do two things at once—greet a guest while you're on the phone, for instance—you're in real trouble.

Some people seem to be naturally more organized than others, but I seriously doubt that there's a gene that carries the tendency to make lists. You aren't born with a follow-up system or an efficient way of remembering what time it is in Paris or the ability to set up a luncheon meeting for thirty people in less than a week. These are skills that you learn from experience, your own and other people's. Everyone I spoke to about this said she had a mentor or two when she was getting started. If you need help in getting organized, find someone to show you the ropes.

Testing

At the Duncan Group we ask our candidates to take a battery of tests, starting with typing and steno, and then moving on to tests for spelling, vocabulary, grammar, proofreading, reading comprehension, analytical ability, and number perception. The whole procedure takes about three hours, and by the end of that time we have a pretty good idea of the strengths and weaknesses of each applicant. I'm not going to reproduce all of the tests in this book, but I want to show you some of them—Spelling, Grammar, Vocabulary, Proofreading, and Decision Making—so that you can get an idea of what I see as the standards for this job. If you'd like to see how you rate, so turn to page 149, Appendix 1. Good luck! (The answer keys begin on page 173, Appendix 3.)

Putting It All Together

The longer you work for an executive, the more discretionary judgment you will be expected to exercise as part of your job and the more "managerial" you will become. As his alter ego and his buffer to the outside world you'll have to take initiative, make decisions, and solve problems. As you learn the job and hone your skills, your boss will become increasingly dependent on you, which means that you'll become even more valuable. He'll need you less for your ability to type than for your ability to think.

In the next chapter I'll talk about how to land one of these great jobs.

3

The Job Search

A N enterprising executive assistant I met some time ago told me about the time she decided to take the matter of finding a terrific new job into her own hands. She ran an ad in the Sunday paper.

DO YOU NEED SOMEONE WHO CAN MOVE MOUNTAINS?

If you're a stressed-out executive with a mountain of work, I can help you. I have excellent skills, including typing, steno, word processing, phone work, a knowledge of office protocol, a little bookkeeping, and a lot of common sense. If you want someone with a good track record and enough energy to leap tall buildings at a single bound, let's discuss.

Her phone practically rang off the hook. The skills her ad described and the creativity and drive it took to run the ad in the first place proved to be an irresistible combination.

Of course, there are a few other, more traditional ways of stalking the perfect job.

Want Ads

Newspaper ads that spell out who, what, when, where, and how much per year are excellent sources of employment opportunity, but blind ads can create major problems. How would you feel if you answered an ad in the newspaper and it turned out that you were applying for a job in your own company? It's happened. As a matter of fact, it's a wonder it doesn't happen all the time. If you're unemployed, blind ads don't present much of a problem, but if you have a job, you'd be foolish to take the chance of answering one.

Employment Agencies

Don't be surprised if, when you answer an ad that appears to have been placed by a company, it turns out to come from an employment agency. The good news is that employment agencies have a vast network of contacts, and they know about more jobs than you'll ever hear about through the grapevine. They move fast, and if you're willing and able, they'll send you out on enough interviews at enough different companies to give you the lay of the land in a hurry.

The bad news is that they don't always tell the whole truth and nothing but the truth in their ads, they usually know less than they should about the jobs they send you out for, and they're far too eager to persuade you to lower your standards, not to mention your price. Many of them don't really understand the nature of what an executive assistant does.

The bottom line is that some agencies are better than others (the quality varies tremendously from city to city), and if you get a good, knowledgeable counselor assigned to your case, you may well get lucky. Here's a word or two of advice if you work with an agency: Before you go out on an interview, insist on hearing a full job description and don't let them talk you into anything that's even one step lower than the level you originally had in mind. They can't waste your time if you don't let them.

The Grapevine

Every business has its grapevine—an information network that makes satellite communications look like the horse and buggy. Your friends in the business can be more helpful than all the want ads and employment agencies combined. That's one of the many reasons it's a good idea to get to know your colleagues, people who have your job in other companies, at least on a professional level if not on a best-friends basis. One group of women I know has formed an informal group of executive assistants who get together once a month to exchange information and tell one another their troubles. Once in a while they put one another onto a new job. It's not just executives who benefit from networking.

Letters

It's a long shot, but once in a while you can get a job by writing a letter. First, it has to go to the right place, of course. Sending it to Human Resources is, in almost all cases, like throwing it down a deep well. In many companies the number of letters that comes from people inquiring about employment is absolutely staggering. Your best bet is to send it directly to the executive you want to reach. Second, it has to be a pretty special letter, one that grabs his attention, stimulates his imagination, and makes him think that if there isn't a job for you, he should give serious thought to inventing one.

I've heard of a few instances when this worked like a charm, such as the woman who wrote a letter that began, "I'd like you to take a few moments out of your day and get creative with me" and went on to explain how much better his life would be if he had her working in his office. It's not the kind of letter that would appeal to everyone, to be sure, but it did the trick with him. She started working for him a few months later.

Choosing the Right Field

One executive assistant told me that early on in her career she worked for the executive vice-president of a company that manufactured fire alarms, vacuum cleaners, and parts for the Polaris missile. As she puts it, "I didn't have an engineering thought in my head then—in fact, I still don't—but it didn't matter at all. I thought it was the greatest job in the world."

Another assistant has had half a dozen jobs in all sorts of fields, and now she works in the fashion industry. "For the first time in my life I'm working for a company that makes a product I can really relate to," she said. "It makes a good job even better."

Yet another assistant, when asked whether it's necessary to be interested in the business of her employer, responded immediately: "I suppose it would be nice, but it's not necessary. I can work anywhere, as long as I like the people and I'm not bored."

To some degree or another, I agree with all three of them. It's by no means essential to know how to build a car to work for Lee Iacocca. On the other hand, if you do have that job, it is to your benefit to know something about how the business works and especially the goals of the business itself. One executive assistant who changed industries, going from broadcasting to advertising, said that she had to adjust her thinking radically. "When I worked for the president in my old job, everything focused on running the company. Nothing was more important than what was going on inside. Here the company is important, of course, but it's the outside client who comes first. I had to shift gears in a hurry."

One of the benefits of being an executive assistant is that if you're a good one, you can work almost anywhere for anyone in any business. If you have even a passing interest in any field— fashion, banking, advertising, law, whatever—you should have no trouble finding a suitable place there if you make that your goal.

34

How to Write a Résumé That Sells

Someone I know who works in a management consulting firm gave me the best advice I ever heard about writing a résumé. "When you're looking for a job, you're selling yourself," he told me. "Think of your résumé as an advertisement." I've regarded résumés that way ever since. To me writing a résumé is your way of presenting yourself on paper.

Back then my experience with résumés mostly involved preparing them for my own purposes. Today, because of the nature of my business, I spend much of my time looking at and evaluating other people's résumés. I think I've seen it all by now—everything from the food-stained and functionally illiterate to the impeccably conceived and professionally printed—and I've come away with some strong ideas about what a résumé should and should not do. As you prepare to write your "advertisement," consider the following elements.

Neatness

A résumé should be clean, neat, and perfectly typed, without any spelling mistakes or typographical errors. I know people who won't consider seeing a person whose résumé is sloppy or inaccurate in any way, and I must say I don't blame them. There's no excuse for a badly typed résumé, especially from a person who includes word processing among her skills. Type and proofread your résumé carefully; then ask a sharp-eyed friend to have a look.

Quality

There is nothing wrong with résumés that are elaborately printed on the finest paper; if you want to spend the extra money to make an impression, that's your choice. However, I'm perfectly happy to see one that is clearly reproduced on good-quality bond paper.

Beware of anything that verges on the flashy, such as colored paper or sepia ink. To be on the safe side, choose white paper and black ink.

Format

I used to think that the traditional résumé format—a one-page listing of the jobs a person has had in reverse chronological order—was the only way to do things, but a few years ago I changed my mind. That was when I got my first terrific two-page résumé. The top sheet (which I've reproduced here) listed the candidate's office skills, and the second page (which I haven't shown) was the traditional year-by-year career history.

OFFICE SKILLS

Typing 95 wpm; shorthand 100 wpm; very computer literate.

*   Office Management and startup: syndication/investment corporation. Personnel recruiting/hiring/supervision; administrative supervision and assistance; computer network, file systems, correspondence, investment product records; due diligence preparation, organization, accounting, prospectus proofreading; office machine lease and purchase; customer liaison.

*   Administrative assistance to chief executive: national charitable and human care organization. Calendar management, travel arrangements; Board of Directors coordination and contact, minutes; community contact at all levels from the Mayor to top corporate CEO volunteers to agencies to donors; regular office duties.

*   Correspondence and reports—self-created and dictated by others.

36

* Project administration and research; museum setup and maintenance; historical documentation and published writings.

* Real estate development office management and administrative assistance; commercial project administration (computerized accounting databases, corporate accounting, budgets vs. actuals, materials purchasing/control); personnel hiring and supervision.

* Top level executive secretary and administrative assistant responsibilities; file system setup & maintenance; corporate/partnership/individual matters; domestic and international.

* Foreign documentation translation proofreading; foreign customer relations (correspondence and phone); exports.

* Computerized accounting database, computerized spreadsheets, budgets vs. actuals, sales records, inventory control, library maintenance.

* Heavy computer experience.

* Public contact at all levels—phone, correspondence, and public speaking.

Obviously this page of Office Skills could not stand on its own, but it offered a way of looking at the person that the traditional résumé didn't provide. I was very impressed by the creativity the applicant demonstrated; it seemed to me that a person who could create that résumé would probably make an outstanding executive assistant. I'm not saying that hers is the only way; I see many traditional one-page résumés that impress me very much. I *am* saying that there is more than one way to skin a cat. You have to consider your background and think about what you hope to accomplish with your résumé and then make up your own mind about the best way to make your case.

Content

Regardless of format, your résumé should tell the reader something about your educational background, including high school, college and secretarial school if any, and any additional courses you've taken that have some bearing on your ability to do the job. The rest is given over to a description of your skills and your career history.

You should include the name of the company you worked for, the kind of business it is (as in Acme Industries, widget manufacturer), and the name and title of your boss. Within each entry explain, clearly and concisely, what your job consisted of, being as specific as possible. "Administrative responsibilities" tells me nothing; I want to know the actual tasks you performed, such as "phone work, letter composition, extensive client contact, scheduling, management of employer's portfolio, travel preparations," and so on. Be sure to explain your supervisory role in the office if you had one and point out any special skills, such as accounting, computer literacy, or a second language. Some of the tasks may seem too small to mention, but I encourage you to include everything. Balancing the boss's checkbook may seem like a little thing, but little things can mean a lot.

What You Don't Say

Many people include "career objectives" on their résumés, but I'm against it. First of all, the objectives people list are almost always so vague and general, they don't mean much. Second, I think that stating a specific objective limits your possibilities. Why take the chance of saying that your objective is to land job A when job B, which would be perfect for you, is right around the corner?

I also don't think that a résumé is a place for listing hobbies and other outside interests. As you'll see in the interview section, which comes next, I believe it's important to know how a potential employee spends her leisure time, but I don't think she should put it in writing. (I heard a story about a hobby listing that came back to haunt an applicant. She included cycling as her hobby, and it turned out that her potential boss was a very serious cyclist. He was all set to have a nice long conversation about technique, equipment, and the various courses each of them had ridden. The problem was, her idea of cycling was pedaling her three-speed down to the shopping center.)

Another thing that you should be prepared to talk about in an interview that's not necessary to include on your résumé is your reason for leaving an earlier job. Potential employers are happiest when people spend four or five years in a job before moving on; if you have a history of job-hopping, be ready to explain why. If you have an especially good explanation, such as following one boss from company to company, you should include it in your cover letter.

Cover Letters

One of the most rude and offensive things you can do in business is send something, anything, through the mail without a cover letter. It's a lot like walking up to someone on the street and sticking something into his hands without any explanation. When you mail your résumé, always enclose a letter with it, and take as much care with your letter as you do with your résumé. Make it short but ingratiating and persuasive, explaining who you are, how you come to be writing and sending your résumé, and why you'd be perfect for the job.

References

I have mixed feelings about references. On the one hand, I know that they're not always very reliable; after all, a candidate is not very likely to offer as references the names of people who are going to say something bad about her. On the other hand, I would never hire someone without checking references very carefully.

When you're job-hunting, somewhere along the line you will need to furnish the names of people who will vouch for you, usually three personal and three business references. These names don't belong on the résumé itself, but in the interests of efficiency I suggest that you prepare a separate sheet with names, addresses, and phone numbers. Be sure to ask people's permission before listing them as references, and if you know in advance that someone will be calling your references, give them some warning. Keep in mind that these people are doing you a favor; don't be too generous with other people's time.

The Job Interview

A woman I know was being interviewed for a job as assistant to the director of a large metropolitan hospital. It was obvious to her right away that the executive was the absentminded professor type. Charming and a little rumpled, he greeted her, asked her to sit, and took his place behind a desk piled high with papers. He began to sift through some of the papers, saying, almost to himself, "Let me see. I have some notes here about what I'm looking for. If I can find them, I can explain to you what I need."

My friend the interviewee couldn't help but smile. "Dr. X," she said, "let me tell you what *I* think you need." Ten minutes later he offered her the job.

Interviews are full of surprises, both pleasant and unpleasant. Résumés speak volumes about a person and references help, but there's just no substitute for meeting a potential employer or employee face-to-face. Knowing how to handle yourself in an interview is critical. Here are some tips on how to make a favorable impression.

Look professional. If you need to refresh your memory about what this means, turn back to chapter 2. You should be clean, neat, and impeccably dressed, just as you would be your first day on the job.

Watch your body language. Sit straight (but not rigid) in your seat, leaning forward slightly to show that you're engaged in the conversation and looking your interviewer in the eye. Don't fidget, shake your foot, twirl your hair, play with your pen, or do anything else to show how nervous you are. Watch the interviewer's body language, too. If he's leaning forward, he's probably interested. If he's fidgeting or leaning back in his chair, you may be losing his attention.

Don't get too comfy. When you're being interviewed, you should be relaxed but not too relaxed. Never ask for coffee or anything else to drink, and if something is offered to you, decline with thanks. Don't be lulled into familiarity by an interviewer who tells jokes and acts as if he's your buddy. He can afford to let his guard down; *he's* not being interviewed. Keep your distance and maintain your own relaxed but formal style.

Mind your manners. Shake hands firmly when you meet and when you leave. Call the interviewer "Ms. X" or "Mr. X" unless you're specifically asked to do otherwise. Wait until you're asked to sit down before you take a seat.

Don't talk too much. Answer questions candidly and openly to the best of your ability and then stop. Don't answer questions you haven't been asked. Don't gossip or tell indiscreet stories about previous jobs.

Tell the truth. It's perfectly acceptable to answer questions in a way that shows you to best advantage—in fact, you'd be crazy not to—but lying in an interview is a big mistake. At the Duncan Group we check practically everything a candidate says, and we're not alone in this. Many employers routinely verify educational background, job history, references, even police records. It doesn't pay to lie about even the most mundane matters either. Don't say you're a theater buff or are mad about the ballet unless you're well versed enough to talk about your so-called passion. Don't say you love to travel if you haven't been anywhere.

Be ready to dodge hard questions. Do you live with someone? Do you plan to have a family? What are your child care arrangements? What are your plans for marriage? Were your parents born in the United States? How old are you? Are you pregnant? Do you belong to a union? Have you every received psychiatric care? According to the Equal Employment Opportunity Commission, these are all questions that a prospective employer has no right to ask. If you're asked something you don't want to answer, simply say, "Is it really necessary to talk about this? That seems like an inappropriate question to me." An employer has a right to know something about you, but you also have a right to protect your privacy.

However, you should understand that if you're too guarded or too defensive when you're being interviewed, you run the risk of giving the impression that you have something to hide. It's impossible to establish any kind of rapport with an interviewer unless you're prepared to open up at least a little.

Close the sale. If the résumé is your ad, the interview is your sales pitch, and as any salesperson will gladly tell you, a sales pitch isn't worth very much unless you remember to close the sale. Here that means asking for the job. This can be difficult to carry off, so it pays to have a little speech prepared, something along the lines of: "Before I leave, I'd like to say that I think this job sounds wonderful. It's exactly what I'm looking for. I really hope that you'll decide to offer it to me." Then follow up the interview with a short note, thanking the interviewer for seeing you and repeating what you said about wanting the job.

Surviving the Q and A

I'm sorry to say that I can't tell you how to answer all the questions that will be put to you during a job interview, but I can give you an idea of what you can expect. In addition to the standard résumé data you are likely to be asked some or all of the following:

- What are your short-term objectives? Long-range? You can be quite specific about the former, but it's best to describe the latter ("What do you expect to be doing in five years?") in more general terms.
- What do you look for in a job?
- What qualifies you for this job? Don't talk for too long here, and always use your most powerful ammunition first. Even if interviewers appear to be paying rapt attention, they often tune out a few minutes into your answer.
- Why do you want to work here? Know something about the company or at least the industry. You can learn much of what you need to know by reading public relations brochures, but sometimes it pays to go to the library and do some additional homework.
- Why are you leaving your present job? Be careful not to say anything negative about your current employer. You may think that those kinds of stories make you look good, but they don't. Nobody wants to hire an indiscreet executive assistant.
- What are your strengths? Weaknesses?
- Which features of your previous jobs have you disliked?
- Describe a situation in which your work was criticized.
- How do you spend your leisure time? What was the last book you read? Movie you saw? Sporting event you attended? If you're like a lot of people, your mind goes blank when someone asks these questions. Be prepared.

- What interests you most about this job? What interests you least?
- Can you work under pressure? Describe a crisis you handled well.
- What are your biggest accomplishments on your present job? How about in your career so far?

Answer all questions candidly and without hesitation, but be careful not to make your answers sound rehearsed.

Questions You Should Ask

Interviewing is a two-way street. When you're being interviewed for a job that interests you, you shouldn't be shy about asking a few questions of your own. The more you can find out up front, the less likely you are to have some unpleasant surprises later. It's crucial that you find out exactly what will be expected of you on the job. Is it strictly clerical? Will you be expected to travel with your boss, to work evenings, to balance his checkbook, to type his daughter's term papers? You have a right to know.

Here are a few questions to get you started.

- Can you tell me something about your job and your role in the company?
- How do you envision your assistant's role? Is she expected to make decisions and be involved in every aspect of your job, or are her responsibilities more limited?
- What kinds of personal tasks will be required? Encourage him to be specific. Find out if you'll be called upon to do things for his wife and children as well as for him.
- What would the typical day be like? Do you like to get an early start or do you burn the midnight oil?
- What's your management style? How do you communicate your needs to your assistant? Do you like her to be independent, or do you prefer giving orders?
- What happens when your assistant makes a mistake?

There are more questions in chapter 11, "For Executives Only," in which I describe the process an executive should go through before hiring an assistant.

Salary Negotiation

If your résumé is a hit and the interview goes well, you'll probably be offered a job. That's when you get to the *really* hard part: talking about money. Hardly anyone likes dickering over salary; it's mildly embarrassing to almost everyone and downright distasteful to some.

In the old days there was very little flexibility about secretaries' salaries; if a job was listed at $18,922 a year, then that's what it paid, no matter who took it. That's not true any more, I'm glad to say. Today companies realize that not all secretaries are created equal, and they'll dig a little deeper to find the right person for the job. (In general, smaller firms are more flexible and easier to negotiate with than large companies.) However, in order to convince employers to dig, you have to know a little something about the art of negotiation.

Here are a few tips.

Know what you're worth. In order to negotiate from a position of strength you have to know what the going rate is for most people doing a given job and how your skills and experience stack up against the average. Once you know that, you can have the confidence to say something like: "Mr. X, I'm afraid that the salary you have in mind isn't enough when you consider the job and the background and skills I'll bring to it. It seems to me that $30,000 a year is a much more appropriate figure."

Stay cool. When someone offers you a salary that is less than you're worth, you may be tempted to throw an ashtray at him and walk out in a huff. Don't. If you're going to have any success in a negotiation at all, you have to be calm; you can't take anything personally. If you're disappointed in an offer, just say so.

For instance, if you've just been offered $23,000 a year, try saying: "I must say I'm a little disappointed to hear what you think this job is worth. I was hoping for $27,000, which is what I think the position deserves and my background is worth." Then the ball is in his court.

If the stakes are higher—say you've been offered $35,000—you might want to take a harder line. Try: "I'm very disappointed in your offer. I'll be candid with you, Mr. X. I need to earn at least $40,000 a year, and I believe I'm worth $50,000. I'm prepared to take the job for $45,000. But I won't be happy with less."

And then there's the short version: "I'm afraid that's not enough. I am not prepared to accept this position for less than $45,000."

Look at the total package. Some companies offer terrific salaries. Others are stingy with salaries but make it up in other benefits: vacation, health insurance, 401k plans, bonuses, tuition reimbursement, and so on. If you agree to accept a salary that's lower than you had in mind, make sure you're getting it back somewhere—say, in a guaranteed bonus and a guaranteed review in six months. Don't be overly beguiled by perks, though; it's your W-2 form at the end of the year that really matters.

Negotiate with the boss. Whenever you can manage it, discuss the matter of your compensation with the person to whom you'll be reporting. (You're going to be working closely together, so you may as well get the relationship started on the right foot.) Some bosses don't like talking about money with their assistants; they'd rather let Human Resources handle those things. If that happens to you, it's worth pressing the matter. Look him straight in the eye and say, "Mr. X, since I'm going to be working for you, I would really rather discuss my needs and expectations with you directly." If he doesn't agree, you can either take your chances with Human Resources or look elsewhere for work.

Beware of "company policy." I wish I had a nickel for every time I heard someone say, "Oh, we can't do that," when what they really mean is, "We don't *want* to do that." I don't consider myself to be a particularly radical thinker, but I think that when policies are silly or unjust (as many salary and benefits packages for secretaries clearly are), they're made to be broken. "I'm sure that if the people who established the policy understood my situation, they would make an exception" is a good place to start. Often the people who dictate salaries have no idea of what people actually do.

Be honest about your salary. The sad truth is that even if you're underpaid, the salary you're earning now largely determines what you'll be paid in your next job. Say you're earning $25,000 a year right now, but you think you should be earning $35,000. Even if you're worth every penny of the extra $10,000, you're going to find it very difficult indeed to find someone who will give you what you want. For obvious reasons, it's very tempting to lie about your salary, saying, for example, that you earn $30,000 now and are looking for $35,000. Even if you end up at $32,000 or $33,000, you've still managed to get yourself a nice raise.

I know that this kind of fancy footwork is quite common, but I'm against lying to prospective employers about anything, including money. In this line of work honesty is essential. If a prospective employer finds out that you lied to him, you'll almost always be disqualified.

4

You and Your Boss

"THE rocks in his head should fit the holes in hers." That's
how an executive I used to work for describes the relationship between an executive and an executive assistant. Other people
have compared it to a marriage or a two-person relay team. However you describe it, there is nothing else quite like the boss/
assistant team. In this chapter I'm going to examine this unique
relationship and offer some insights about how you can go about
establishing one that works for you and your boss.

Chemistry

Chemistry—that word comes up without fail whenever I talk to
an executive assistant about her relationship with her boss. "I
could never work for someone unless I felt some connection with
him" is the way one puts it. "I wouldn't work for someone I
dislike, no matter how much the job paid," says another. When
two people work as closely together as an executive and his assistant, there is a kind of intimacy that one doesn't often see in
professional relationships. I am not talking about sexual intimacy;
as you'll discover later in this chapter, I am very much opposed
to a sexual relationship between an assistant and her boss. I'm

referring to a closeness that is built on trust and mutual respect and shared goals. I realize that this is a strange way to describe a situation in which one party is likely to out-earn the other several times over, but it's nonetheless true. In many ways an assistant is an extension of her boss.

The chemistry that comes with a good boss/assistant relationship (or a solid marriage, for that matter) means different things to different people. "If he's fair and reasonable and smart, I can put up with almost anything," one assistant told me, and I'm sure many would agree with her. Others might be a little fussier. When I asked several executive assistants what they look for in a boss, I discovered that the answers broke down into the following categories:

"I have to respect him." No one expects perfection in a boss, but all executive assistants need to feel that they're working for a person who is doing something that matters. "I don't have to love him, but I do have to believe in him and respect what he does. Otherwise I can't work for him" is a comment I've heard often.

"He has to respect me." An assistant is not the equal of her boss in the eyes of the company (if you aren't sure, just compare their W-2 forms), and it would be foolish to pretend that she is. She works for him, and he is her superior. That doesn't mean, however, that she is not worthy of respect for what she does for him. Even if they don't hear about it every hour on the hour in so many words, assistants need to know that deep down, their bosses have a high regard for their work and consider them able, intelligent co-workers.

"The way I look at it is, we're partners," one assistant said. "I make him look good. That's my job and my pleasure. In return I have to have a good salary, excellent benefits, and some acknowledgment that what I do matters around here. I don't make $250,000 a year, but I'm smart and very good at what I do. I couldn't bear being treated as if I were stupid."

"I want him to treat me like a human being." I've heard stories of executives who almost never speak to their assistants, not even to say, "Good morning" or "Good night," let alone "Please" and "Thank you." Many executive assistants don't seem to mind a boss who keeps his distance. One assistant I spoke to, who had worked for a few especially abusive executives in the past, said it didn't bother her one bit. "I suppose it would be nice if he greeted me in the morning or asked if my cold was better, but I really don't mind being ignored," she said. "Frankly, I'd rather have him ignore me than drive me crazy with criticism the way my last boss did."

Most people I talked to need a little more attention than that. One woman spoke for most of her colleagues when she said, "I just need my boss to recognize that I'm a person, too, with a few needs of my own. I don't mean that he has to ask to see the pictures of my kids or the slides of my vacation, but I do expect him to remember that I *have* kids and to understand that I need a vacation once in a while. It's important for me that we connect on some human level."

"I don't like being taken advantage of." There isn't an assistant alive who hasn't felt put upon at some time or other, but everyone I talked to said that you have to know where to draw the line. "On the Friday of my first week on the job my boss dumped a presentation that needed three hours' worth of work on my desk at 4:30, told me he had to have it first thing Monday morning, and then walked out to play golf. The presentation had been sitting on his desk all day, but he waited until the last minute to give it to me. Of course, I had no choice but to stay until 7:30 to finish the report, but I didn't appreciate his thoughtlessness. What made it even worse is that on Monday morning, he didn't even mention it.

"A few days later when he did the same thing I appreciated it even less. By the time he did it the third time, I realized that he was enjoying himself; I guess it made him feel important to control my life like that. I finally got up the courage to tell him that I was having some problems with his system, but I didn't get anywhere. I finally just had to leave."

Most assistants are more than happy to work overtime when it's necessary, but they are all mindful that there is a fine line between meeting the demands of a job and bearing the brunt of an abusive employer.

"I need some consistency." Executives are human, and as such they have as much right to change their minds as the rest of us. No assistant should expect her boss's desires and expectations to be the same, day after day. Still, she does have every reason to object when his behavior is erratic or he is unreasonable—when he wants his mail handled one way on Monday and another way on Tuesday and then back the old way on Wednesday, for example.

One assistant told me about an executive for whom she had been working for over a year who pulled the rug out from under her one morning. "This is going to sound silly, but it really threw me for a loop. I had been typing his letters for a year, and one morning he came to me, really quite angry, and said that he absolutely hated the way his letters looked. Since they looked exactly the way they had been looking for a year, I couldn't imagine what he was talking about. It turns out that he wanted me to start putting the date on the left margin instead of the right. Of course, I made the change, but I thought the whole thing was pretty weird."

A few manifestations of this kind of "weird" behavior are perfectly acceptable, even common, and you have to learn to accept them as part of the job. If they start happening all the time, however, it's probably time to find a new job.

"He has to have integrity." Everyone I spoke to expressed this opinion to some degree or another. Assistants want to work for someone who is fair, who has good values and a keen sense of

proportion, and who keeps his word. This goes for his dealings with the outside world as well as with her.

"He has to be smart." Almost all the people I spoke to mentioned how important it is for an executive to be intelligent. "I have to feel I can learn from him" and "He's taught me so much, not just about business but about other things" are comments I've heard repeated over and over again. I agree completely. One of the most important aspects of an assistant's job is the opportunity it gives her to grow and learn within the job. During my years as an assistant I learned about Japanese prints, real estate values, geography, and French wine, among many other subjects. Because the executives I worked for had a great many interests and enthusiasms and because their activities were so varied, I couldn't help but pick up some expertise along the way.

Working for a genius can be wonderful, but it can also be a real handful. There are plenty of geniuses out there who are very difficult to work for; many are absentminded, bad-tempered, or ill-mannered—or all three. One assistant who works for a brilliant but impossible executive told me that she wouldn't pass up this opportunity for anything. "If you want to see how his mind works, you have to accept the whole package," she said. "To me it's worth it."

"I've got to have feedback." Almost everyone agrees that working for someone who doesn't tell you what he wants is a nightmare. An executive assistant's job is hard enough without having to include Mind Reader on her job description. As one woman puts it, "It's not that I need my hand held, but every once in a while I need to know whether things are going well. Is he happy? Am I doing what he wants? Should I change anything? A boss who never says anything makes me crazy."

"I need to know that he'll always back me up." I've saved this until last, but in some ways it should be at the top of the list. An

executive has to be able to trust his assistant to do whatever is right and necessary to help him get his job done. By the same token, an assistant has to perform her job with the understanding and confidence that she has her boss's support.

I remember very well a time when my boss was tested and passed with flying colors. One of his vice-presidents failed to get a report in on time. My boss wanted it on Friday afternoon, but the VP turned it in first thing Monday morning. Even worse, he lied about it, telling my boss that he had delivered it on time but that I must have forgotten to pass it along. Naturally my boss asked me about it, and I told him the truth, that the report was late and the VP was lying. I'm glad to say that the level of trust between us was such that he believed me—he knew that if I said I got the report Monday morning, that's when I got it—and he told the vice-president so. That kind of support is essential if an executive assistant is going to be able to function effectively and happily.

The list above is long, but it's definitely not complete. I hope it inspires you to think about what kinds of satisfaction you need from your job. Before you can establish a solid working relationship with your boss, you have to understand what you are looking for. It will help if you also understand that the person you work for won't be perfect. That's all right, though, because you aren't perfect either.

In chapter 3 I talked about the kinds of questions you should ask before you take a job, in order to avoid unpleasant surprises, but the truth is, you can't really know someone until you have worked for him for a while. Don't be ruled by your first impressions; they can be way off. You need to give it some time before you decide if you two are going to hit it off. I've learned that some of the best executive/assistant matches have gotten off to a rocky start. If after giving the matter careful consideration, you conclude that the chemistry is really wrong, then you can make plans to leave.

Communication

When a boss/assistant relationship is really good, there is almost a special code between them. He hardly has to say anything. "He'll give me ten words of instruction, and I turn it into a thousand," one assistant told me. If there is to be proper communication between you and your boss, you have to know what is expected of you. And you have a right to make your own needs understood.

Most executives are pretty set in their ways; they like things done their way or not at all, and it's highly unlikely that anyone is going to get them to change. Once in a while an assistant can sand off the edges a little by showing her boss new, improved ways of getting things done. If you're new on the job, however, don't just plunge in and start making suggestions. Wait a while, take your boss's measure, and note how the organization works. Once you've done your homework, you can feel free to rock the boat, ever so gently.

I learned that lesson the hard way several years ago, just after I had started a new job. In my previous job the man I worked for was "Mr. Follow-Up": when he sent a letter to thirty executives asking for a response on a certain day, he expected me to be on the phone reminding people the first thing in the morning on the day the responses were due. What's more, he wanted me to talk directly to the executives, not to their assistants. In the middle of my second week on the new job I tried the same thing and almost started World War III. The phone lines from a few of the executives to my boss were practically smoking, so angry were they that I had the audacity to call them directly and make "unreasonable" demands. Obviously, Mr. Follow-Up's ways were not accepted here. In my eagerness to be efficient, I had neglected to learn the nature of the relationships at the new company. It would have been a simple thing to ask my boss how he wanted me to handle his follow-ups. You can be sure I asked a bushel of questions after that.

It's all very well to recommend that you talk to your boss, asking him questions and keeping the lines of communication wide open, but that's usually a lot easier said than done. I've had some of my most meaningful conversations with my bosses as I chased them down the hall or rode in elevators. On one dark day—when I had to pin my boss down about his travel schedule in the next half-hour or else—I loitered outside the men's room waiting for an audience.

To keep this sort of thing from being necessary too often, try to set aside some time every day to talk, ideally in the morning, at noon, and at the end of the day. Then make those minutes count by being prepared with a written agenda. When you do finally corner your boss, make certain that you're not getting him at a bad time. If he's just returned from a meeting at which a presentation he worked on for days was not well received and you can see he's in a bad mood, don't press him to make a decision. Use your head.

If you're new on the job and just "breaking in" a new boss, keeping the lines of communication open can be a little daunting. One assistant I spoke to still laughs about the time almost ten years ago when she was a rookie assistant. She had been working for her new boss only about two weeks, and he was about to set off for London on the company plane. She asked him what he'd like to have to eat on the flight; he chose the shrimp platter with a side dish of broccoli. She put the order through, and sure enough, that is what he was served about an hour after the flight took off. The only problem was, it was time for breakfast.

"I thought it was an unusual thing to have for breakfast, but I was too shy and nervous to question him about it. For all I knew then, he had shrimp and broccoli for breakfast every morning!"

Anticipating His Needs

It's impossible to say what the most important part of an executive assistant's job is, but if really pressed, I would probably say that it's knowing what's important to him and anticipating his needs.

In order to be a top assistant you have to know what makes your boss tick. You have to know what he cares about, what he's a real stickler for, and what drives him crazy. Then you must do whatever is necessary to make your boss comfortable.

Most of the time anticipating his needs means taking care of commonplace business matters: paperwork, phone calls, meetings, travel plans, and so forth. However, some of the time, it means catering to his whims in matters considerably more trivial.

As any executive assistant will tell you, bosses care about some pretty strange things. There's the man who wouldn't read anything unless his assistant put it on the left side of his desk; another insisted on having his assistant's desktop set up exactly like his; and the man who couldn't start a meeting in his office until he took everything off his desk. Then there are the stories about the man who couldn't work if the pictures on the wall were crooked; the one who had to have a dozen brand-new pencils every morning; and the one who made his assistant wrap a package three times before he was satisfied with it. One executive in the throes of a huge takeover deal spent an hour on the phone one morning arranging to have new frames made for the artwork in the office lobby.

Laugh if you want to; in fact, I recommend it, especially if you end up working for one of these people. But after you've finished laughing, remember that the things that seem unimportant can be critical to your boss's peace of mind. If it's important to him, make sure it becomes important to you.

I heard a story recently that illustrates this point very well, although the person telling it meant to make another point entirely. A woman who works for the president of a music production company was told by him to set aside a block of tickets to one of his concerts for several of his friends. She got the tickets and distributed them to the boss's guests, but as everyone discovered on the night of the concert, the seats were terrible. Her boss, embarrassed in front of his friends, was furious at her.

"I can't believe he got mad at her for something so trivial," the storyteller said to me. "She thought the seats were good. It wasn't her fault."

I disagree. The assistant, who had been working for the executive for over a year, knew very well that her boss was fussy about just this kind of thing. She understood perfectly how important it was that he look good in front of his friends. She should have made it her business to check out the seats in advance.

Criticism

Once in a while you make a mistake, and you have to be prepared to take the consequences. Some bosses yell and carry on. Others get quiet, *very* quiet. ("Some people think that because my boss is quiet, he's not really mad. Boy, are they wrong," an assistant told me.) If there is a problem with something you've done, your boss has a right to tell you about it and to insist that you change your ways; however, that right does not extend to public humilation. He should have his say in private and express himself in a respectful way.

If I live to be two hundred years old, I'll never forget the time someone I worked for called me into a meeting and said, in front of a roomful of people, "Melba, I can't believe you made such a stupid mistake!" All I could do at the moment was turn on my heel and leave the room; I certainly wasn't going to dignify his disgraceful behavior by responding to it. Later I confronted my boss, telling him that if he ever did that to me again, I was leaving. From that day on he kidded me about how thin-skinned and sensitive I am, but he got the message. He never criticized me in public again.

Private Needs

One late afternoon the CEO I worked for was on his way to the airport to catch a flight to Florida, and I got a frantic call from him over the car phone. "Melba, I'm desperate," he began. My heart sank. "I don't have my golf shoes. Could you please get them from the closet in my apartment and meet me at the airport as soon as you can?" I grabbed my coat and made tracks to his apartment. Within fifteen minutes I was rummaging around in his clothes closet. It was only then that I realized that I didn't know what golf shoes look like. I called a friend, received an education in golf footwear, and was soon on my way to the airport with my prize. It was all in a day's work.

I guess you know by now that there is a lot more to being an executive assistant than typing, filing, and answering the phone. The true job description of most assistants also includes one or more of the following: balancing the checkbook, paying bills, picking up dry cleaning, and sending oatmeal cookies to his daughter at college. In my time I've typed the boss's wife's thesis, tracked down his runaway dog, hired a driver, and, in an emergency, taken his tennis shoes in to be resoled. What's more, I didn't mind doing any of it.

As far as I'm concerned, these tasks and plenty of others like them are all part of the job. In fact, many people will tell you that handling personal needs is the most critical part; after all, "anyone" can type a letter, but not everyone possesses the ingenuity it takes to get a French visa in less than twenty-four hours or the judgment required when the boss's son calls from Europe with an emergency. Private needs are so important, it's not at all unusual to find executive offices in which there are two assistants, one to handle business, the other for personal matters.

Much has been said about how it's beneath the dignity of secretaries and assistants to make coffee or otherwise cater to an executive's personal needs, but I strongly disagree. These kinds of tasks are demeaning only if you think they are. No one can make you feel used if you refuse to let him. If you are paid well and treated with respect and if you have self-esteem, you can perform such seemingly unimportant tasks with satisfaction, even pride. You don't have to love it, but you shouldn't regard it as punishment.

One young assistant only a short time out of secretarial school told me, "It doesn't bother me to make coffee. Believe me, it's a lot more fun than lining up at the Department of Motor Vehicles for two hours, which is what I did last week. It's all part of being an assistant."

Of course, it's important that these kinds of personal tasks not be sprung on you out of the blue. An assistant has a right to know before she takes a job what will be required of her along these lines (see chapter 3). It is also her prerogative to call time-out when she feels that she is being badly used. Every assistant I've ever talked to has something she won't do, no matter what. For instance, I would never pick up after my boss; I once worked for someone who had a habit of dropping things on his office floor, no doubt expecting me to pick them up and put them away or throw them in the trash. When that didn't happen (I was prepared to let the stuff stay on the floor until it rotted), he eventually broke his habit. When an executive assistant I know was asked to clean out her employer's closets, she put her foot down. She and her boss had a long talk and set some important limits.

If and when you have that talk, try saying something like: "I am uncomfortable doing this. I think it adds a dimension to this position that I wasn't expecting. If this is something that you expect me to do, we need to talk about it. I'll be glad to do it this time, but next time I think it would be better for me to arrange for someone else to do it. I'll supervise."

If the chore itself is not unacceptable and what worries you are the time constraints, try, "I don't mind typing your wife's report, but let me tell you what else there is to do. I need your help in deciding what I should do first."

I believe that people who categorically refuse to perform personal tasks on the job are limiting their opportunities. There are some great jobs out there, but most of them involve finding a pair of golf shoes now and then. One veteran assistant I know said it very well when she told me, "Sure, I make his coffee, and I keep his ice water pitcher filled all day. I even wash out the cups if I have to. My twenty-four-hour beverage service has become a joke around here. To tell you the truth, I don't like that part of my job at all, but I do it gladly. It's not as if I'm his servant. I work for a wonderful, fascinating man, I make terrific money, and I have one of the best jobs in the world. I'm sure not going to throw it all away over a cup of coffee."

Confidentiality

If you're the kind of person who can't live without office gossip, don't become an executive assistant. I'm not very keen on office gossip for anyone, but it's absolutely out of the question for someone with this job. You don't have to be a master lexicographer to notice that the root of the word secretary is *secret*.

It's not always easy to keep your own counsel in an office, and occasionally it can seem downright antisocial. It's no fun cutting a conversation short with "I'm afraid I have nothing to say about that" or "It's completely inappropriate for me to discuss this" or "You must know that there's no way I can talk about that," but that's what you have to do. I've heard it said that the major drawback of this kind of work is that it's difficult to have friends at the office. Many women who work for CEOs find that having to watch what they say all the time puts them under so much of a strain, they prefer to keep to themselves at the office.

Some matters are so sensitive, you can't talk about them even with your boss. "I open his confidential mail, but I usually pretend I never even saw it," one assistant told me. "If he wants to talk about it, he can bring it up." This is the way most people I talked to handle knowing top secret information.

Your title may not be *secretary,* but you are nonetheless a keeper of secrets. Your days of hanging out at the watercooler are over.

Loyalty

When questioned about her role in Oliver North's infamous paper-shredding operation, Fawn Hall described herself as "an experienced and devoted secretary who did what I was told and did not ask questions." This "I was just taking orders" posture insulted the good name of secretaries everywhere. The role of a secretary is to be supportive, yes, but support does not demand duplicitous or unethical behavior. You shouldn't have to cheat or steal or break the law to do your job well, and no one has a right to expect it of you.

A boss has no right to take advantage of your trust and good faith by asking you to do something dishonest or to lie for him, in either his business or his social life. For example, if he's having an affair, that's his business; it's out of line for him to involve you in any of the subterfuges to which he might have to resort. For one thing, an assistant often has a relationship with her boss's wife and children. It's cruel and unusual punishment to ask you to make hotel reservations or send flowers to his girlfriend one minute and talk to his wife about their plans for the evening the next.

Socializing with the Boss

"I had worked for months putting together a fund-raiser for my boss, so I was really pleased that he invited me. It went beautifully—cocktails, dinner, everything. It was black-tie and all very glamorous. I had never been to a party with so many rich and famous people; it was lovely to be introduced to people I knew over the phone. I felt a little bit like Cinderella. Then, as the party was just about over, my boss walked over to me and said something like: 'Mr. Y is coming by the office first thing in the morning. Don't forget that he likes corn muffins with his coffee.' In a matter of seconds my coach had turned into a pumpkin."

I sympathized with that young executive assistant's sad story, because the same kind of thing has happened to me a few times, too. It's probably happened to every assistant who lets herself forget her real role for even a moment. There will be plenty of people who will disagree with me, I'm sure, but I have always felt that attending functions like the one the young woman described—luncheons, dinners, cocktail parties, and assorted galas—is not all it's cracked up to be. I avoided them whenever I could, and when I couldn't, I made a brief appearance and then beat a hasty retreat. Assistants just starting out may enjoy the adventure of meeting the great and near-great, but more experienced ones come to understand that, all things considered, you are often better off declining with thanks.

One woman who's been through the assistant wars told me, "I used to like to go to these things, but I got tired of being a guest one minute and an employee the next. It was just too stressful. Besides, I have my own friends. I don't need to go to parties with his."

There is nothing wrong with mixing business with pleasure, provided you understand what you may be letting yourself in for. You are, first and foremost, your boss's employee. If you lose sight of that fact, you'll regret it.

Working for a Woman

In May of 1988 *USA Today* reported the findings of a Purdue University study that examined management behavior. Two of the things they discovered were: (1) women managers are more democratic than men (men tend to be more autocratic); and (2) people believe that women managers care more about people than about getting the job done (men are thought to care more about the job than the people).

I'm not sure what those findings mean, if anything. I'm not even convinced that they're true. What's more, I confess that I'm a little reluctant to bring up this subject at all. The idealist in me wants to insist that women executives are the same as men, that there is no difference whatsoever in working for one or the other. However, the realist in me, the one whose business it is to identify and meet various needs in the workplace, knows that there is a prejudice among some assistants against working for a woman executive. I don't fully understand the reasons behind that prejudice, and, for obvious reasons, it doesn't make me very happy.

Theories abound about why women find it hard to work for other women: women are "used to" serving men, but it seems "unnatural" to serve another woman; women who have gotten ahead have to be aggressive, which means that they're rough on the help; or women can't happily work for someone with whom they identify. For all I know all of these theories have some validity, but in my opinion they don't add up to anything you can take to the bank. The story with women executives is the same as it is with men executives: There are some great bosses out there and some real stinkers. I believe that it pays to look for a good woman boss, because there are advantages in working for a woman. For one thing, women understand other women in ways men never can. For another, a female executive can be a real role model for an assistant. And finally, helping another woman succeed can only mean good things for women in general.

Still, I meet executive assistants every week who walk in to my office and say, without batting an eye, "There's no way I'm going to work for a woman." I change their minds if I can—mostly I talk about how they're limiting their opportunities—and accept their decision when I can't.

A woman executive's needs are much the same as a man's, but there are a few special considerations to keep in mind when you work for a woman. Women in business often are fighting the stereotype of being helpless and dependent, so our lives must be set up to counter that. When I travel, I need to feel independent, and that means feeling safe and in charge. I want reliable transportation and secure accommodations. I need to know my schedule every step of the way. No one likes to wander around in the middle of the night looking for a cab in a strange city, of course, but women need to take unusual precautions.

Even now, in the very late 1980s, the issue of "Who's going to pick up the tab?" when a woman executive entertains is still very much with us. When I have lunch or dinner with a business associate, the fact is I don't really care who pays (although I do think that the unwritten law that the person who does the inviting pays makes a lot of sense). I do care about being spared the embarrassment of assuming that the other guy is paying when he's not or offending a companion by taking out my credit card when he expects to pay. When there is some doubt about who's paying, an assistant can be very helpful by asking a few discreet questions in advance, when a lunch or dinner is being arranged. "Will you be hosting the lunch?"; "In whose name shall I make the reservation?"; "Shall I make the reservation in Ms. Duncan's name?" are all gentle ways of finding out beforehand who will be paying the bill.

Sex in the Office

They may not look like it, but offices can be sexy places, filled as they are by lots of people working closely together, sometimes for many hours at a time, eating meals and traveling together. It's not surprising, then, that once in a while one thing leads to another. For all that, I think sex in the office is less common today than it used to be. I know that the cliché of the secretary sitting on the boss's lap is largely a thing of the past. If I had my way, it would disappear completely and for good.

Perhaps I should have called this section "No Sex in the Office," since I believe that if you want to sleep with the boss—even if you're single and he's single and yours is the greatest love story of our time—you shouldn't work for him. If you fall in love with your boss and he falls in love with you, you should leave.

In the first place, an affair will wreck your working relationship. How can you have a relationship with someone that's private and sexual and then take orders from him the next day? In the second place, it makes you a laughingstock in the office. If an executive assistant is going to be treated with the respect the job deserves and requires, she needs to conduct herself professionally and with dignity. When the people in the office find out that you're sleeping with the boss (and don't kid yourself, they *will* find out), you can kiss your dignity good-bye.

For your own sake, keep your relationship with your boss strictly business. Don't abdicate that responsibility to him; you have the most at stake, so it's up to you to make the rules. Conduct yourself properly, without even a hint of flirtatious behavior. If anyone makes a sexual overture, make sure that he understands clearly that he's out of line.

Crazy Bosses

The best boss is the one who respects his assistant, who communicates with her, challenges her, and gives her room to grow. If life were perfect, all executives would be paragons like that. But it's not, and they're not. The terrible truth is that most intelligent, high-powered bosses are difficult, sometimes *very* difficult. I've talked about the crazy little things that can mean a lot to an executive. Here I want to address the subject of the boss whose behavior is truly intolerable. I've met some, heard about many, and even worked for a couple myself along the way.

The kinds of people I mean are abusive and nasty. They like to holler and swear at their employees. They enjoy humiliating people and making them squirm. Some of them even get physical; I talked to a woman who had a stapler thrown at her by her last boss (she was out of there before it hit the ground, I'm glad to say), one whose boss cut the heads off her plants, and to another who, when she finally quit, was afraid to turn around and walk out for fear of what her employer would do. Other impossible bosses are the ones who abuse you psychologically—lying, flaunting their wealth and power, or blaming you for their mistakes. I once met an executive who had seven assistants in one year. Knowing as I do how much most assistants will put up with, I shudder to think what life with him must have been like.

You can't reason with these kinds of people. When confronted with complaints about their behavior, many bosses act as if their accuser is imagining things or overreacting: "You know I don't mean anything by it when I shout. I didn't know you were so sensitive."

Every pot has its cover, they say, and it's probably true. I imagine that there is an assistant willing to work for even the craziest boss. In my view, however, there is no reason to work for someone who is abusive, not even if you get "combat pay." You have to know when to quit. One assistant who prides herself on her professionalism told me a story that still makes her blush. After only a couple of weeks on a new job, she called her boss and quit without notice. "He was a terrible man, very abusive, and I thought his business practices were repugnant," she explained. "I just couldn't bear to do the job another day."

I don't blame her a bit.

PART II

Office Protocol

I N part 1 I described what I see as an excellent career opportunity and explored the unique relationship between an executive assistant and her boss. Now, in part 2, I'm going to get down to the nuts and bolts of being an executive assistant, concentrating on how to do the job efficiently, professionally, and with a minimum of anxiety. The strategies I offer come from my years on the job and from the experiences that my colleagues shared with me. As you do the job yourself, you will no doubt discover new, improved ways of getting various tasks done, but in the meantime, here are the secrets of my success.

5

Working the Phones

YEARS ago I worked for an executive who was constantly being called on the telephone by people he didn't know. Hardly a day went by without his hearing from a stockbroker, an insurance or real estate salesperson, or some other businessman or businesswoman who was trying to fill a daily quota of "cold calls" to high-ranking executives in *Fortune* 500 companies. Most of the callers were straightforward and honest about why they were trying to speak to him, and I often either arranged for them to talk to my boss or referred them to other, more appropriate members of his staff. Every once in a while, however, I'd get someone who had a hard time taking no for an answer.

I remember very well one man who asked for my boss by his first name and, when I asked who was calling, said he was an old friend and this was a personal call. Now, after working for this man for several years, I was fairly certain that I knew the names of all his friends, and I had never heard of the caller. When I asked how they knew each other, the caller was vague, referring to business school years ago and a recent conference that had brought them together again. My instincts told me that the man was lying. I was pretty sure that he was just trying to sell my boss something.

I probed a little more deeply, inquiring about the nature of the call and volunteering to take a message, but the man continued to take evasive action. I asked for his number, explaining that my boss was busy and would have to get back to him at a more convenient time, but he said he was traveling and couldn't be reached. The man called again later, and again he wouldn't leave a number. Finally, when he called a third time and I made it clear to him that unless he left a number, he was never going to get to speak to my boss ("Mr. X has specifically asked me to get a number where you can be reached" is how I put it), he finally broke down and gave it to me.

Of course, I proceeded to do what any sensible executive assistant would do: I dialed the number. It was just as I suspected all along; the operator answered with "Good morning, XYZ Insurance Company." My next step was to get the caller on the line and give him a piece of my mind. "You have dealt dishonestly with this office," I told him. "You claimed to be a friend of Mr. X, but in fact you are trying to sell him insurance. We have no interest in the way you conduct business, so please don't ever call here again." I'm glad to say that he never did.

My reaction to the salesman's business tactics may seem a little extreme, but I was doing one of the most important parts of my job: handling the phone. In this particular case I was protecting my boss from a caller who was out to waste his time, the kind of thing I did—and any executive assistant does—a dozen times a day.

Knowing how to work the phones is one of the most important aspects of an executive assistant's job. If you know how to handle people and can learn to do it quickly and with skill, the telephone can be your greatest ally, as important to you as an electronic typewriter, the most intricate word processor, or a well-sharpened pencil. Phone skills can make or break a top secretary.

Much of the business we do at the Duncan Group is done over the phone—talking to clients and candidates—and everyone who works with me knows how fussy I am about telephone skills. No one handles the phones until he or she is comfortable in our environment and knows our system cold. If you think that I'm exaggerating the importance of phone skills, keep in mind that the assistant's voice, *your* voice, is the first thing a caller hears when he calls an executive's office. As the "first line of defense" in an office, you project an image and set a definite tone, and in many cases you even speak for your boss. A secretary's behavior on the telephone may not determine the course of business relationships, but it can have an enormous effect on them.

During my career as an executive assistant I must have spent at least 75 percent of my workday on the telephone, and I probably still do. Here are some of the strategies I have learned through experience.

Sounding the Part

The telephone is an incredibly sensitive receptor. True, no one can know how you look when you speak on the phone—even if your office is on fire you can still sound all right—but unless you make a conscious effort to modify your voice, most people will know exactly how you feel. All sorts of emotions can be detected in the voice. If you are tense or confused when you pick up the phone, there is a good chance that you'll sound tense and confused. If you're stressed or angry, the caller will probably know it.

It is critically important for an assistant to sound as if she always has things completely under control. No matter what sort of day you're having or how many other calls are on hold, every time the phone rings you must sound comfortable with your surroundings and as if you know what you're talking about. Even if you are surrounded by chaos, you have to give the impression that you are cheerful and in control.

A few specific ways to sound in control over the phone are:

- Answer the phone as quickly as you can, preferably right after the first ring. The longer the phone is allowed to ring, the more harassed and disorganized you appear to be.

73

- Don't sigh into the phone as you pick it up. This is very common practice, and it almost always conveys a negative message to the caller, as if you're too weary or too hassled even to listen to what he has to say. To get things off to a more positive start, take a deep breath when the phone rings and smile as you pick it up and greet the caller. If you smile, you will automatically communicate your enthusiasm to the caller.

- Modulate your voice. If you are to make yourself understood and be treated with the respect your job deserves, you must speak in a pleasing manner, without excessive regionalisms, enunciating clearly and using the proper tone of voice. A grating voice or a tendency to mumble or speak too loudly are made even worse on the phone. If you suspect you have a problem with your telephone voice, do something about it. (See chapter 2 for more about correcting speech problems.)

- Don't talk with your mouth full of food. It's perfectly all right to have lunch at your desk—in fact, many executive assistants don't have time for anything else—but spare your callers the accompanying sound effects. Stop chewing before you answer the phone.

- Finish your conversation before you pick up the phone. Some people believe that it makes them sound busy and important to continue talking to someone in the office as they answer the telephone. That may be so for tycoons, but it makes executive assistants sound disorganized. Don't pick up the phone until you've stopped talking.

- Remember that hold buttons are there to be used. If you have to put someone on hold, do it; don't just cover the mouthpiece with your hand and carry on a conversation. Neglecting the hold button is professionally indiscreet, not to mention impolite.

- No matter who the caller is or what the call is about, your manner should be firm but not arrogant. Convey to the caller the sincere message that you care.

Mastering Salesmanship

In order to communicate effectively over the telephone, you basically need a sales mentality; you are, in essence, selling yourself to the person on the other end of the line. This is especially true when you are asking people for help or trying to convince somebody to tell you what you want to know, such as who he is and why he's calling and what he wants from your boss.

Sometimes this is easy, but once in a while selling yourself can be a problem, especially when you are talking to people with a "you're just a secretary, so you can't possibly understand what I'm talking about" attitude. I'm talking about the people in business who think that assistants are too stupid or just too unimportant to be trusted to convey even the most marginally complicated information or message. The way they see it, they simply *have* to talk to the boss.

The only way to go about converting such people is to sound confident, efficient, and knowledgeable about what you're doing, to be persistent in your efforts to persuade the caller to trust you, and to remain calm but firm in your resolve to get your job done. Whatever is said you have to keep your cool and remain professional, being as ingratiating as you can manage. I can remember many conversations in which I had to prove myself to a skeptical caller who wasn't too happy to be dealing with the "help."

"It's just too complicated to leave in a message," the person would say. "You had better have Mr. X call me directly so that I can explain the situation to him."

"I'm afraid that the only way Mr. X is going to get the message today is if you give it to me," I would reply patiently. "So why don't we give it a try?"

Establishing the Ground Rules

Find out from your boss exactly how he would like you to answer the phones in the office. Personally I like "Good morning, Mr. X's

75

office," but some executives would rather have you skip the "Good morning" part. Others prefer "Chairman's office" to the use of their names. If your boss has no opinion, use your own judgment.

After you have settled on a satisfactory greeting, the next important item that you and your boss should discuss is who is on his "A" list—that is, which of his telephone callers are to be put through to him automatically, without questions from you. People on an executive's "A" list are usually family members, senior management staff, the company's board of directors, important outside consultants, and perhaps a few friends. Then there is the "B" list, which is composed of the names of people whose calls must be returned the same day they're received; this list often includes bankers, lawyers, accountants, brokers, and close personal friends.

You should also have a clear understanding of the types of callers who should be referred elsewhere and those that should be handled by you. You and your boss should also have a general agreement about what constitutes an emergency. It's one thing to be protective of an employer; it's quite another to withhold information that he may need. I always worked for executives who were delighted to be spared phone calls and wanted me to screen callers thoroughly. (Of course, I kept a record of each call and an account of its disposition, and once a day I would fill my boss in on the various calls he had missed.) Not every executive feels the way my employers did.

It's impossible to provide for every contingency in advance, of course, but if you and your boss discuss his accessibility in general terms, you will be better able to cope with questions and problems as they arise. Some bosses like to have open-door policies in their offices; they enjoy being available to employees and other business associates. Others rely on their assistants to shield them from the world. The sooner you discover which kind of boss you're working for, the better.

Finally, you should ask your boss if there is a message-taking style he prefers; by the time someone in business reaches an executive level, he has probably developed strong opinions about systems, and there is really no way of knowing what he likes unless you ask him. Some like the traditional pink slips for phone messages; others like all calls on one sheet; others opt for somewhat more eccentric systems. One of the executives I worked for liked all his messages written on individual stickers, so that he could move them around at will. This worked well most of the time, but every once in a while I would discover a stray phone message stuck to his sleeve.

Because it is essential in the Duncan Group offices that the right hand always know what the left hand is doing, we swear by the telephone call sheet, which describes every call that comes in to the office and includes a description of its disposition. (To see what it looks like, see chapter 6.)

Placing Your Boss's Calls

Virtually no executive likes to answer his own phone—too many unpleasant surprises there—but many are perfectly willing to take charge of their outgoing calls, dialing the phones themselves. (This system works beautifully, provided your boss tells you about the calls he has made or returned.) Others want no part of the phoning process at all and expect their assistants to handle the chore. Obviously it's up to you to find out which category your boss falls into.

Placing calls is a simple, straightforward matter; when the assistant on the other end answers, you simply say, "Mr. X is calling for Mr. Y. Is Mr. Y available to speak to him?" or "Mr. X is returning Mr. Y's call. Is Mr. Y in?" If Mr. Y isn't in, you leave a message. If he is in, you put your boss on the phone and congratulate yourself on a job well done. There's nothing to it—unless, of course, you are sidetracked by a small skirmish in the Telephone Wars, also referred to as "Who Gets on First?"

I can't tell you how many times I did battle with another

executive assistant about which of our bosses was going to get on the line first. "Okay, Melba, put him on," my colleague would say when I told her that my boss was indeed in. "Sorry, you called me. Put him on," was my reply. On a good day one of us would give in quickly, but once in a while stubbornness would get in the way of efficiency. There we were, two grown women with responsible jobs, squabbling over telephone turf.

The unspoken rule is that the person who makes the call should get on the phone first. (If they call you, wait for Mr. Y to pick up and quickly say, "Mr. Y, one moment, please. Mr. X is picking up right away" and then make sure your boss does so. If you keep Mr. Y waiting, chances are *your* boss will have to wait the next time.)

Screening Calls

If you ask a hundred executives what their idea of heaven is, I'm sure that a substantial percentage would say, "Never having to talk on the phone again." In an ideal world an executive would never have to take a telephone call; his assistant would handle all of them, running interference between him and the people on the other end of the phone. The fact is, a good executive assistant can handle virtually every phone call made to her boss, but before you can handle a call, you have to find out who is calling and have some idea of what the person wants. That is sometimes easier said than done.

After you have worked for someone for a while, you come to recognize most of the voices you hear on the phone and you know enough about the business itself not to have to give everyone who calls the third degree. However, until you do know the ropes, screening your boss's calls—that is, helping him to avoid people he doesn't want to talk to and to communicate efficiently with the rest—can be quite tricky. You have to start with the confidence that comes with knowing that this is part of your job; this is what your boss pays you to do. You're not just being nosy when you ask people questions. You're being an efficient and professional executive assistant.

Many people save you the trouble of asking who they are by identifying themselves up front, but if they aren't considerate enough to do so, you have no choice but to ask. Saying, "Who is calling, please?" may seem a little blunt, but as far as I am concerned, it's the best way to find out what you want to know. ("May I tell him who is calling, please?" is a popular version of the same thing, but to me the words "tell him" create the impression that your boss is in. If he isn't, or if he is but he doesn't want to take the call, you have dug yourself a hole that can be awkward to climb out of.)

If a caller is reluctant to tell you his name, you have every right to insist on his giving it to you. Sometimes it's necessary to say something like, "I'm sorry, but Mr. X has specifically asked me to tell him who is on the phone before I put a call through to him. If you want to speak to him, you'll have to give me your name."

Once you have the name of the caller, you have another decision to make. If you have no idea who the caller is and don't know if your boss wishes to take the call, you need to do some further investigating. Many assistants who are looking for information say something like, "What is the call in reference to?" but that sounds stilted and a little cold to me. When I am trying to find out why someone is calling, I think it's a little nicer to say, "I'm sorry, Mr. X is terribly busy today, and he's not taking calls at the moment. Can you tell me the nature of this call?" A variation on this theme is, "I'm afraid that Mr. X has ten calls to return and then he has to go directly into a meeting. Can you just give me an idea of what it is you would like to speak to him about?"

Keep pushing until you have the information you need to make a decision but don't be arrogant or rude. Let the caller know that you're on his side, that you want to help him get what he needs or wants from your boss. Somewhere along the line you are bound to come across someone like the insurance salesman I described at the beginning of this chapter—a person who isn't honest about who he is or why he is calling. If and when that happens, you have my permission to express the annoyance you will undoubtedly feel.

Once you know who the caller is and the reason for the call, you must respond. Whatever your reply is, it's important that you don't sound as if you're struggling to think of an answer or, even worse, telling a lie. For instance, "I'll see if he's in" sounds like a lie to me. Since you are bound to know whether or not your boss is in unless you are very inefficient indeed, what the statement really means is, "I'll see if he wants to talk to you," which is pretty rude. There is no reason to offend a caller or make him feel slighted even if his call doesn't get through to the boss.

If you know that the executive you work for doesn't want or need to take a call, make a polite excuse that sounds plausible and gives you some flexibility: "He's on another line, and there are several calls waiting"; "He's behind closed doors, and I don't expect to be able to speak to him for the rest of the morning"; "He's out of the office for most of the day"; or just the vague "I'm afraid he's not available" are all trusty excuses. (There is no law that says you have to tell a caller where your boss is or what he is doing there.) If you can handle the call yourself or transfer it to someone else who can, so much the better.

If you aren't sure whether your boss wants to speak to the caller, buy some time and find out. When you get the caller's name and the reason for the call, say, "Oh, Mr. Y, please hold. I have another call." After you've conferred with your boss, come back to Mr. Y and give him your answer.

Keeping the Caller Informed

No matter how you look at it, being kept waiting on the phone is a pain in the neck, but I have always felt that waiting is a lot easier to take when you know exactly what you're waiting *for*. In our offices we never say, "Good morning. The Duncan Group. Please hold." At the very least the person who answers the phone finds out the caller's name, makes a note of it, and says, "I have another call. Please hold." Even if there are ten calls at once, there is always time to find out who's calling before you ask the person to hold. Then, after all the calls have been quickly taken, you go back to the calls in the order they came in.

When you do make your way back, use the caller's name and offer a brief explanation of why the delay was necessary. "I'm sorry to have kept you waiting, Mr. Y, but I'm afraid there were several other calls ahead of you. I can put you through to Mr. X now." Or, if you can't put the caller through, you can say, "Mr. Y, it looks as if Mr. X will be busy for most of the afternoon. May I help you with something in the meantime?"

There are times when your boss is busy but you know he's been waiting for this call. Again, tell the caller what you're going to do before you let him hang on the end of the phone. "Mr. Y, Mr. X is on another line at the moment, but I know he wants to talk to you. I need to put a note in front of him, and it may take me a few moments. Can you hold? Thank you."

Or try something even more dramatic: "Mr. Y, I know Mr. X needs to talk to you, but I have to ask you to wait for a few moments, please. I have three calls holding, and then I have to go down the hall to get him. All that should take about three minutes."

Then, before you put the call through, tell the caller what you're about to do. Get back on the line and say, "Thank you for holding, Mr. Y. Mr. X will speak to you now." Putting the call through without announcing your intentions can catch the caller off guard.

If you're transferring a call, tell the person why you're doing it and to whom he is being transferred, including the new person's extension, just in case the transfer doesn't work and the caller gets lost. It's important not to let a caller feel snubbed or shunted aside. If the transferred call was really important, follow up.

If you're about to lose an important call, share the specifics of your boss's schedule with the caller if you think that will help: "He's traveling today, but he'll be calling in from the airport at three this afternoon. Is there any way I can reach you at that time?" Find out the caller's plans for the rest of the day. Get his home phone number. Find out where he's dining, how late you can call in the evening at home, and how early he'll take calls in the morning. Convey how eager your boss is to speak to him and do whatever it takes to make it happen.

I have told some elaborate stories in my time, particularly on hectic days, when I knew that if I let a caller go, I would spend the rest of the day trying to track him down again. (I distinctly remember begging on a few occasions.) I'm glad to say that I didn't lose many of them, and I think that's because I took care to keep the caller informed so that his wait was as comfortable as possible. That kind of concern makes all the difference in the world.

Minding Your Manners

I'm a little old fashioned when it comes to telephone manners, and I'm not ashamed to admit it. I like courtly and formal behavior in the office. I'm happy when people say "please" and "thank you" and otherwise mind their manners. I can't remember ever feeling badly treated on the phone by someone who was overly polite. On the contrary, I am often horrified by the casual manner I see and hear, even in some of the top executive offices around the country.

The most important thing to remember when you speak on the phone is that the persona you project has little or nothing to do with you; it is a reflection of the person you work for. It doesn't matter if in "real life" you are a great raconteur with a sparkling wit. It doesn't count that you love to gossip or enjoy hearing the details of the exploits of other people's children. When you are at work, you speak for your boss, and that means maintaining a high level of restraint and decorum, no matter how much you are tempted to do otherwise.

Here are some specific things to remember about proper telephone etiquette.

Skip the slang. You'll never be taken seriously if you end every sentence with "okay?" or "right?" or a nervous giggle. Pay as much attention to your language when you speak as you would if you were writing the words down. Use complete sentences, with a logical train of thought. Speak with firmness and authority, using the King's English. If you have to make a particularly difficult call and you're nervous about getting it right, write what you want to say on a piece of paper and read it. Speaking well is a habit; the more you do it, the easier and more natural it will become.

Don't waste time. Whether you're giving information or taking a message, keep the conversation short. Without being rude or abrupt let the caller know that you don't have time for chitchat.

Keep your distance. For some people being friendly but not too friendly is one of the hardest parts of the executive assistant's job. Extremely gregarious people find this especially challenging. One woman I've worked with is constantly having to rein herself in, since her natural inclination is to get a little too chummy with her boss's clients. Unless she is careful, a casual "How are you?" has a tendency to lead to a lengthy chat about the client's daughter's forthcoming wedding. Unfortunately this kind of intimate chat simply won't do, and it's up to you to discourage callers from pursuing it. Be courteous, but keep all conversation professional.

Don't lose your temper. And then there are those callers who are *un*friendly, even angry or hostile. Again, it is essential to maintain your equilibrium. Never let a dissatisfied customer rattle you so much that you lose your professional demeanor. Remember that when you're on the job, you are speaking for your boss. Don't speak in anger or raise your voice. Stay calm and encourage the caller to calm down as well. If things get out of hand and he becomes truly abusive, say, "There is no point in continuing this conversation" and gently hang up.

Don't call people by their first names. In a business environment, even in the late 1980s, I still believe that men should be called Mr. and women should be referred to as Miss, Mrs., or Ms. No matter how casual your office is, you should never use anyone's first name unless you are specifically invited to do so. Keep in mind that being called by *your* first name does not constitute an invitation; many people's attitudes are such that they automatically call assistants by their first names, but that doesn't mean you should follow suit. (Some assistants bring it on themselves, saying, "This is Mary in Mr. Smith's office" when what they should say is, "This is Mary Jones in Mr. Smith's office." Even a "lowly" secretary deserves to have a full name.) Continue to use the more formal address even when faced with someone who doesn't.

Don't fight fire with fire. You can control your own behavior, but there is not much you can do when others misbehave. The first time a certain cabinet member listened to a message I had for him and then, without saying a single word, not even goodbye, simply hung up the phone, I admit I was a bit perplexed, but of course, I wasn't rude to him in return. (I later learned that he does that to all assistants, not just to me.) I continued to be polite whenever I had occasion to call his office. And believe it or not, I eventually got used to his peculiar way of treating underlings.

Juggling Calls

If you're a fan of old movies, you've seen the stereotypical scene of the switchboard operator faced with dozens of ringing phone lines. If the movie is a comedy, she probably ends up with some of the wires wrapped around her neck. Well, modern technology has put an end to the switchboard, but that doesn't mean that the problem of what to do when several phones are ringing at once has gone away. Now we have the hold button.

In the first secretarial job I ever had my boss had two lines, and there were times during my first week of work that I thought I'd never get the hang of the phones. Juggling calls on line 1 and line 2, particularly if I was in the middle of typing a letter, was almost more than I could bear. Ten years later I was working for a top executive with twenty phone lines, and on most days I handled them without blinking an eye. What made the difference in my attitude, of course, was experience. Juggling phone calls is not really something you can learn very well in the abstract. It's the sort of skill that requires some serious on-the-job training. Rehearsal can be helpful—I've been to seminars in which role-playing sessions proved to be quite useful to beginning secretaries—but all things considered, you have to experience "phone mania" to know what it's really like.

Whether you have two lines or twenty, the routine is the same: You answer the call and find out who it is, making a note if you can't trust your memory; explain the situation to the caller and put him on hold; and get back to the caller as soon as possible. In general I think it's a good idea to handle calls in the order they come in, but naturally, if you get an urgent call, it should take precedence over the others. In this as in all things, you have to use your common sense.

Try this for size: "Good morning, Mr. X's office. Who's calling, please? [Make a note of the name.] Mr. Y, I have three other calls waiting. Will you hold for a moment, please? Thank you." The whole exchange takes less than half a minute, and then you're free to handle another call.

In some instances, when the phones are ringing off the hook and you know you can't give a caller the attention he needs and deserves, you may be better off not putting the call on hold. "Mr. Y, I have three other calls waiting, and I don't want you to have to hold. May I call you back in fifteen minutes?" Most people would rather busy themselves at their desks for fifteen minutes than spend five minutes on hold. Be sure that you keep your word, though. If fifteen minutes come and go without a call from you, the caller will have every reason to feel slighted.

Following Up

In a perfect world all phone calls would be returned by the end of every business day, but unfortunately the world isn't perfect. More often than not there are many calls left unreturned at the end of the workday. Despite your best intentions and those of your boss, some people are going to be disappointed. When this happens, make a quick interim phone call yourself: "I'm really sorry, but Mr. X's schedule was crowded today, and he's not going to be able to speak to Mr. Y after all. Tomorrow looks good, though." If you think that it will be a few days until he returns the call, say so: "He's going to be out of the office for most of the next few days, so I can't promise that you'll hear from him until Thursday or Friday." With luck you can handle the call yourself by passing messages back and forth.

The follow-up call is just one more way of demonstrating that you take the needs and demands of your job seriously and that you care about the people who call your office.

6

Shuffling Paper

I once asked a colleague, one of the most accomplished and experienced executive assistants I've ever met, what salient words of advice she would pass on to young people breaking in to the business. She answered without hesitating even for a moment: "Never go anywhere, not even to the water fountain, without a pencil and paper. You never know when you're going to have to write something down."

When I pressed her for a little more about what it takes to be a truly top executive assistant, she said, "To do this job well you have to be able to handle people and paper." In this chapter I'm going to concentrate on paper—the various kinds you are most likely to encounter and the most efficient way to cope with it in all its forms so that it does you and your boss the most good.

What my friend said about the importance of handling paper was no exaggeration, by the way. When an executive assistant is not juggling calls on the telephone, she's likely to be handling some form of paper: memos, letters, spread sheets, calendars, annual reports, checks, itineraries, and the like. I once had a boss who used to make important notes to himself and to me on restaurant matchbooks. As part of my daily ritual I would go through his coat pockets looking for matches and do my best to decipher what was written on them.

Some boss/assistant relationships are based almost completely on the exchange of paper; a particularly busy executive or one who travels a great deal is not very often available in the flesh. An assistant can go days without seeing or talking to her boss except for brief exchanges on the telephone. Another of my colleagues, one who manages a secretarial staff of four for a *Fortune* 500 CEO, says that she meets with her boss for a half-hour at eight o'clock every morning, but after that she's unlikely to speak to him again for the rest of the day. They communicate by writing notes.

I have said before and will say again that when you do this job, you can't be scatterbrained. You need the ability to concentrate on what you're doing, and that means knowing what and where everything is in the office. You probably know the cliché about the person with the impossibly messy desk who knows exactly where everything is. Well, I'm not suggesting that you need to keep a messy desk, but I do think that you have to become a genius at sifting through paper, getting the gist of its substance, and committing the necessary facts to memory.

Probably the greatest challenge in an executive assistant's life is the volume of paper that she is expected to read, absorb, file, and retrieve. There is no question that it's pieces of paper shuttling back and forth that keep most businesses afloat. Let's take a look at the kinds of paper you're likely to encounter.

The Mail

Being in charge of opening an executive's mail, which is included in the job description of every assistant I've ever come across, is a mixed blessing. On the one hand, it can be an overwhelming task; I've had jobs in which the stacks of mail that arrived every day literally covered my desktop and took an hour to sort. On the other hand, it's an essential part of your job; you can't be effective in your role as assistant unless you are aware of the pieces of paper that come into and go out of your boss's office. You can't anticipate your boss's needs if you don't know what is going on, and you can't know what's going on unless you open the mail.

Unless you are told otherwise, assume that opening the mail that comes to your boss is part of your job. One exception is mail marked "Personal" or "Confidential" or both. You'll probably end up opening mail in those categories as well, but you must wait for your boss to tell you to do so. Usually he will, although it may take him some time to make the decision; after all, there is very little in his business or even his personal life that you don't eventually get involved in. Even so, don't take it upon yourself to open his personal correspondence. Wait until he gives you explicit permission.

Everyone has her own preferred method of sorting the incoming mail. In my days of opening executives' mail I would begin by putting every piece of mail in one of the following piles: Immediate Attention, Deadlines, Information, Invitations, and Junk. Then, before I passed it along to my boss—usually in folders marked "Read immediately," "Read in transit," and "Read and toss"—I handled everything that could be handled by me in advance. On any given day that might mean drafting replies, declining invitations, clearing schedules, making suggestions as to the disposition of a request, gathering information that I knew he would need before he could respond to a letter, or even highlighting important points in what might have looked like junk mail. Often I would make a note of the name of someone else in the organization to whom I thought a letter should be passed on for handling. (This is yet another reason it is critical for an assistant to know who does what in an organization.)

This sort of initiative is the mark of a good assistant, but you can have too much of a good thing. In your efforts to stay one step ahead of your boss and anticipate his needs, you have to be careful not to get carried away and overstep your bounds. Make sure to keep your boss informed every step of the way, whether you're turning down an invitation, sending along a brochure, or answering a question from a client. When your boss runs into a colleague who says, "Too bad you couldn't come to the luncheon last week" or "Thanks a lot for passing along that article" or "I'll see you next month in Zurich," you don't want him to be in the dark about what the other guy is talking about.

After going through the mail, my bosses returned most of it to me, some of it noted with responses or instructions, others with a simple check mark, which meant, "Noted. Please file." My mail-handling system worked well for me and my employers, but you'll probably want to invent your own mail plan, one that best suits your boss's temperament and the type of business you're in. Anything that works for you is the "perfect" system.

The Calendar

During a meeting with an executive assistant I placed in a chairman's office a few years ago, I asked her to talk about the systems she and her extremely busy boss have settled on to keep his schedule running smoothly. "Basically I spend half my day updating all of our various calendars," she said with a smile. "At the moment we're down to four: the daily date book on his desk, my desk daily, his month-at-a-glance calendar, and the little black diary he carries with him all the time. Sometimes I feel like a sideshow juggler, only instead of four balls I have to keep four calendars in the air. Of course, it's a nightmare when he travels. I always ask him to make the changes in his diary, but he doesn't always remember. And every once in a while he makes a date and forgets to tell me. Somehow it all seems to work out, though."

Anyone who works for an executive can sympathize with my friend's tale of woe. Maintaining a calendar can seem like a full-time job. Most people have at least three calendars to keep track of: one on his desk, one on yours, and a portable one that most CEOs would never be without. Once in a while you come across an executive who likes to make all of his own appointments, but that's relatively rare. In most offices the assistant has complete access to her boss's calendar and is free to make and break appointments for him. In addition to the calendars many executives find it useful to have a daily schedule printed on a separate sheet, which they take home with them at night or have waiting on their desks first thing in the morning. Naturally the assistant should keep a copy for herself and make changes in both whenever necessary.

In scheduling appointments for your boss you have to have a sense of timing. In the interests of efficiency you want to cram as much in to a workday as can be effectively managed, but don't forget that most things take a little longer than you think. Just because most diaries divide the day into half-hour segments doesn't mean that people and meetings do the same. After you've been working for someone for a while, you begin to get a feel for how long his various meetings take. For instance, you might know that if he has an executive committee meeting that starts at ten, you had better leave him free until lunch time. You'll also get to understand the pace that your boss prefers. Some people thrive on being rushed from meeting to meeting; they enjoy having more to do than they can easily manage. Others need a little breathing room between appointments.

(There is a lot more to meetings than writing them down on a daily diary. I talk about the rest in chapter 7.)

Invitations

Successful executives are always being invited somewhere to do something—to a party, a luncheon, a business conference, a banquet, and any number of other gatherings. A certain amount of what I call business socializing comes with the territory of being an executive. I remember a day when one of my bosses received twenty-two invitations. Needless to say, he could not have accepted all of them even if he had wanted to.

It was my job to make sure that he knew about every one of the invitations, to check his calendar in order to determine which ones he was able to accept, and to make the appropriate calls or write letters declining with thanks. Again, I was always careful to tell him about every invitation, even if there was no way he could be there. I would attach a note that said, "I have declined, since you are busy, but you should know about this" or when he did have room in his schedule, "You are free to do this. Yes or no?"

When he was invited to speak out of town, I would always do some research before giving him the choice to accept or decline. I'd get on the phone and start asking questions: What time is he scheduled to speak? How long is the speech supposed to be? When can he leave the hall? Will transportation be provided? One of the executives I worked for disliked having to spend the night away from home unless he absolutely had to; he much preferred getting home late at night to staying in a hotel. For him I was always trying to find a late-night or early-morning flight. Commercial airlines rarely came through, but company planes were often helpful to our cause. I was always careful to ask if there was anyone else flying to a given location on a private plane and if there might be room for my boss. By the time I showed my boss the invitation to speak, he had all the pertinent information laid out in front of him.

This all sounds organized and tidy when it's written out like this, but of course the process isn't always so simple. I have a strong memory of the luncheon one executive forgot to tell me he had agreed to host. Since it wasn't on his calendar, when an invitation came to attend an equally important lunch, we accepted with thanks. When the fateful day arrived, my boss did the only thing he could do to rectify the situation. He ate two lunches.

Phone Messages

In chapter 5, in which I talked about telephone etiquette and described the art and science of managing the hold button, I referred to the telephone call sheet we have come to rely on in our office. As you can see from the one I've reproduced here, the phone log serves as a diary of the day, a kind of permanent record of at least one kind of business that has been transacted that day. It's big enough not to get lost or hidden under something, and to make it even easier to spot we usually keep it on a clipboard. Copies of the call sheet are circulated to several key people at the end of every work day, so that we all have a solid overview of what's going on. It consists of the following repeated several times down the length of a page and includes the date noted either at the top or bottom of the sheet:

TELEPHONE CALLS

am	Name	Message
pm		
To be handled by	Number	
	F/U Status	Date _____

Ours is largely a telephone business, so we would be lost without the call sheet. In my years as an executive assistant I had several bosses who liked the call sheet as well, but a couple of them preferred the more traditional pink sheets, with one phone message per caller. With the one-piece-of-paper-per-call method your boss and you have the satisfaction of wadding up the paper and throwing it away once you've dealt with each call, but the bad news is you also have the anxiety that comes from misplacing a particular pink slip or losing it altogether. Even if my boss liked his messages noted separately, I kept a running list of incoming calls to be returned on one sheet of paper on my desk.

The Rolodex

If my office were on fire, the first thing I would grab is my Rolodex. And I'm fairly certain that most executive assistants would say the same thing, although many of them would really have their arms full; many use two, three, four, or even more card files on a regular basis. In some ways everything you know is contained in those cards; mine contains a lifetime of business knowledge and experience.

My rule was that if I talked to a person more than once, I put his name, address, and phone number on a card in my Rolodex. To save time and confusion later I would always get the exact spelling the first time around, and if I thought it would ever be necessary to reach the person at home, I'd ask for his home number as well. (Once in a great while someone was unwilling to give out a phone number, but ninety-nine out of a hundred were happy to oblige. They knew I had no intention of misusing the information.)

Name, rank, and serial number are only the beginning when it comes to making notes on Rolodex cards. I used mine to record all manner of useful information, including any relevant information about the business he has done with the office, the name of his spouse, and, most important of all, his assistant's name. Then I cross-index the cards, so that if I forget a name, I can find what I'm looking for under "Florist" or "Helicopter" or "Caterer" as well. You have to develop a system that works well for you.

I've always felt that if an assistant really wants to be efficient in her job, she should know the name of every secretary/assistant in town. Saying something like, "Good morning, Ms. Z. It's Melba

Duncan calling for Mr. X. Is Mr. Y available to talk to him?" is so much friendlier and more respectful than treating the secretary (and yourself, for that matter) like a nameless cipher. There are many terrific people I've never met but have been communicating with for years on the phone. Our conversations are always brief— sometimes only "How are you today? Oh, I know exactly what you mean. Is he in for Mr. X?"—but even so, we establish a connection that makes doing business a real pleasure.

Letter Writing

Entire books have been written about how to write a proper business letter, so I won't try to teach you how to do it here. If you are weak in the area of letter writing, I suggest that you consult one of them for a refresher course. Much of the time you'll simply be typing letters dictated by your boss, but there will undoubtedly be occasions when you'll need to draft the letters yourself. Depending on what sort of boss you work for and what your skills as a wordsmith are, you may end up writing as many of his letters as he does.

Letter writing is definitely a challenge, but once I got over my initial nervousness about putting words in someone else's mouth, I used to enjoy drafting letters for my various bosses. It let me exercise my creativity while I eased his burden a little. It also meant getting letters out somewhat more speedily than might otherwise have been the case. I've talked to some executive assistants who write virtually all their bosses' letters, after discussing the contents with them if necessary, of course. One executive I know who tends to be too formal and stilted in his letters counts on his assistant to take the chill off his correspondence and give it the personal touch. Another finds it almost impossible to say no to anything, so he depends on his assistant to do it for him. Yet another has an assistant who writes particularly lovely thank you notes, so he counts on her for that.

You can learn the basics of letter writing from a book, but the only way to get really good at it is to practice. It will require work, and you may have to endure some merciless editing from your boss, but believe me, your efforts will pay off. Writing is a very desirable skill for an assistant; the more "strings to your bow" you can accumulate, the more valuable an employee you will be.

Filing and Paper Retrieval

I've never met anyone who likes filing. There is no way to get around the fact that filing is a dull, tedious job. There's also no way around the fact that it absolutely has to be done, and done well, if you are to do an efficient, responsible job. Some experts maintain that there are three critical elements in an office, all of equal weight: your maintenance of telephone records, your filing system, and your ability to retrieve a piece of paper when it's needed later.

The advent of the computer has revolutionized many office filing systems, but I have to say that while I am a big fan of computerization, I still like the security of holding in my hand a piece of paper that I can copy and file and eventually retrieve. In fact, I make copies of practically everything—letters, enclosures, invitations, phone messages—before I let it out of my sight. My habit got to be something of joke in several offices I worked in, but I let them laugh. Early in my career I had worked for an executive who had a tendency to lose things, and I was determined that it was not going to happen again.

Every office needs three basic files.

Alphabetical file. Each letter your boss writes, along with a description of the specific enclosures that went out with it, should be filed under the recipient's last name (or perhaps the company name or job name). Those files are kept in alphabetical order.

Chronological file. All the letters you write over the course of a day go into a daily "chrono" file, which has a cover sheet listing all the letters in the file. Having the cover sheet, which should show the date the letter was written, the recipient's name, a list of the enclosures, and a brief description of the subject of the letter, usually spares you from having to rummage through the whole file whenever you're looking for something. The last thing I did before leaving for home every day was to make sure the chrono file was complete. It's been my experience that if you let that chore go for even a few days, you begin to lose control of the paper flow. One executive assistant I know hates filing so much that the only way she can bear to do it is one piece at a time. If she lets it pile up even a little, the job becomes almost unbearable.

Tickler file. This is a filing system—some people call it a follow-up file or pending file—that contains a record of matters that are to be followed up on a certain date. The one I used had twelve folders, one for each month, and within each folder there were slots for the days. It was an easy matter to remind myself what had to be done that day. All I had to do was look in the file for that day and take out the various pieces of paper: invitations to respond to, deadlines that had to be met, insurance payments that were due, even birthdays of the boss's kids or prominent clients. All those things and anything else you can think of can be included in a tickler file. No efficient office should be without one.

It's a straightforward enough matter to invent and use a filing system. If you use your common sense to establish logical file categories, you won't have much of a problem tucking pieces of paper away so that they're safe and sound. That's the easy part. Finding them later on is another story.

One of the most stressful aspects of being a secretary is paper retrieval, tracking down a letter or other document after it has been carefully filed. There's nothing quite like being asked by your boss to get a copy of the letter he sent to that man he met in St. Louis a few years ago, the one about the Widget merger, when he can't remember the man's name or when he met him, let alone when he wrote the letter. With luck *you'll* remember the man's name, or at least the name of his company, which is probably how you filed it anyway. Or perhaps you'll be able to recall the month he wrote the letter, so that you can head for the cover sheet in the chrono file. Or perhaps you'll end up spending your day looking for the elusive letter, all the while muttering, "I know it's here somewhere!" I've missed dinner more than once doing just that, and so have most of the executive assistants I know.

In deciding where and how to file material, I always try to imagine the worst thing that can happen—for instance, a letter that is lost forever—and then do whatever I can think of to keep it from coming true. Making and filing several copies of a letter may seem like an unnecessary strain on both you and the office copier, but in the end it will make your job easier, I promise. No one is perfect, of course, and even belt-and-suspenders types like me lose or misfile things once in a while. However, if you take care, it will rarely happen to you. That means taking pride in your work and being concerned and interested in what your employer does. It means making connections. Don't just stick pieces of paper into a file. Read them and understand their significance. If you do that, you'll find it a lot easier to find them later.

Remember, retrieving paper is *your* job, not your boss's. Sure, it would be wonderful if every executive had the extraordinary ability to remember the name of everyone to whom he ever wrote a letter, and it would be fantastic if he also had a great head for dates, but there's a good chance that he doesn't have those skills. It's all up to you.

Lists

I'm a fiend for making lists, not because I'm forgetful but because I'm careful. I believe in Murphy's Law—anything that can go wrong will go wrong—and I also believe in Duncan's Law—

anything that reduces stress and the possibility of error on the job is a Good Thing. To me there is no such thing as being too organized. Writing something down is the best way to insure that I'll remember it. Why clutter up your mind with a list of the groceries you need for your shopping trip after work when all you have to do is take a moment to put them down on paper? That same logic applies to the tasks that face you on the job. My desk would not be complete without my clipboard and my "Things to Do" and "People to Call" lists, which I refer to and update dozens of times every day. Do yourself a big favor and pick up a clipboard of your own.

Inventing Your Own Shorthand

Most boss/assistant teams who have worked together for a while reach a point at which they communicate almost in code. A check mark comes to mean, "OK, file." A question mark says, "What do you want me to do with this?" "FU 1/20" means follow up for a reply on the twentieth of January. All of these shortcuts save time and effort and make it easier for you to do your job. One assistant I've spoken to about the system of communication in her office came up with an interesting solution to a small problem.

The problem was that once in a while her boss was slow in making decisions, or at least in communicating his decision to her. Sometimes she would have to wait days for an answer to the smallest, simplest questions. One day, almost as a joke, she asked her boss a multiple-choice question. She listed the three possibilities as she saw them—*(a)* Yes, I want to go; *(b)* No, I don't want to go; and *(c)* I'll go but only if I can fly back the same day—and asked him to check one. He made his choice and returned the note to her within the hour. And thus a new communications system was born!

7

Coping with Meetings

EVERY executive assistant I know has dozens of job horror stories, tales of planes missed, crucial letters that went astray, and Thanksgiving dinners that had to be kept warm while last-minute revisions to an overdue proposal were angrily typed. Some of the stories are fairly funny, at least in retrospect. For instance, when I think about the evening I sent my boss off in black tie to an affair that called for business suits, I can't help but smile. ("At least you were the best-dressed person there," I said lamely at the time. I'm not sure he saw the humor in the situation.) One of my colleagues had no choice but to smile and shrug when she told me about the day her boss showed up promptly at the New York Stock Exchange for a meeting that was being held at the American Stock Exchange.

Most of the stories are somewhat less comical, of course, especially the one I recently heard from the assistant to an executive who is very active in the arts. He sits on the board of several cultural institutions in Manhattan. She spent two weeks setting up an important meeting with half a dozen movers and shakers in the arts community, including a Broadway producer, a world-famous choreographer, and someone from the mayor's office. Finally, after dozens of phone calls and untold hours of schedule juggling, she was able to put the thing together. The morning of the meeting her boss called in sick, so, of course, she had to cancel the meeting. By the time she finished making the phone calls, she was tempted to go home sick herself.

A lot of the "war stories" you hear from veteran assistants revolve around a part of the job that is positively fraught with peril: meetings. Whether they're held in or out of the office, meetings can throw a major monkey wrench into the works of a well-run office. Organizing life for one person is hard enough. When you try to orchestrate the comings and goings of a group, you are practically begging for trouble.

The typical executive spends a great deal of his workday in meetings, which means that as his assistant you spend a lot of yours arranging them, making sure he gets there on time, interrupting them to give him messages, typing agendas, and making sure there's cream for the coffee if any is served. Let's take the elements one at a time.

Outside Meetings

I've never met an assistant who is truly relaxed or happy when her boss is out of the office. ("I'm not really content unless I can see him!" someone once said to me. And she wasn't kidding.) When the executive is within earshot, you can pretty well control what's going on in the office. Once he leaves, however, all bets are off. Flat tires, traffic jams, lost directions—all those and more threaten to keep him from the swift completion of his appointed rounds.

Again, the key to averting catastrophes, or even minor mishaps, is anticipation. I used to treat this part of my job almost like a game, asking myself what could possibly go wrong. Then I would follow the thought through, coming up with actions I could take either to prevent the worst or to prepare for it when it did happen. All in all, my approach worked well. Once in a while there were surprises, but most of the time I beat the odds.

The extraordinary thing about many executives is that while

they can keep a mass of incredibly important information in their heads, they are perfectly capable of forgetting which floor they work on. Professors aren't the only people who are absentminded. I've worked for executives, brilliant, decisive, talented people, who simply drew a blank when it came to dealing with the relatively mundane matters of daily life, such as hailing a cab, writing a check, or remembering the name of the restaurant where they're supposed to have lunch. The assistant who works for this kind of boss has no choice but to work extra hard to make sure that all contingencies are covered.

Not all of the people I've worked for needed this kind of attention; in fact, some executives proved to be quite independent. With those who needed help, though, I pulled out all the stops, especially when I had to send them out into the world. When one of the absentminded ones left the office, he always had the specific details of his destination written on a large (so he wouldn't lose it) piece of paper. On the paper was the address, complete with cross street, the best entrance and elevator to take, the floor number, and the name and phone number of the person he was to see. If he was traveling in a hired car, I'd also list the number of the car and the name of the driver. If he had his own driver, as many executives do, the driver received a copy of the paper as well. In his briefcase my boss would carry a folder that contained all the details of the meeting to come, including the names of the attendees, the agenda, and any other relevant papers.

Most of the time I would walk my boss to the elevator, where I would personally hand him the paper and put the folder into his briefcase. If I was feeling particularly nervous—afraid that he'd lose something on his way out of the building, for instance—I accompanied him to his car. I often wondered what would happen if I went all the way and pinned a note on his jacket that said, "I'm Mr. X of Acme Industries, 123 Main Street. My phone number is 123-4567. If I get lost, please return me to my assistant."

I realize that I'm making all of these efforts and procedures sound like more fun than they really are. Frankly, it can be anything but fun to deal with a grown man or woman who can run a *Fortune* 500 company, negotiate a million-dollar deal, and make government policy but who can't seem to keep track of his or her own glasses. It's not easy spending time on trivial matters when you have "real" work to do. What's more, there were many times when I got the distinct impression that my boss was being "helpless" on purpose. There's no question in my mind that this sort of helplessness is often an act—after all, why not pretend to need to be taken care of when you have someone who will do it?—but that doesn't make it any less real. Ignoring this you-know-I-can't-do-this-sort-of-thing-myself-so-please-take-care-of-it-for-me attitude doesn't make it go away. Since you can't make it go away, you have to learn to take it in stride.

Some bosses push their demands too far. One executive assistant I know found out (later than she should have) that she was expected to come in every morning, make coffee, and slice and serve a fresh papaya to her boss. After that she was supposed to sit and take dictation while she watched him eat it. If you find yourself in a similar position, you can try to get your boss to change his ways (a long shot to say the least), or you can do what my friend with the papaya-loving boss did: look for another job.

As I discussed in the "Private Needs" section of chapter 4, every executive-assistant job comes with its share of what I think of as babysitting, and if you like your job, I encourage you to accept reasonable demands for what they are—not your favorite chore, perhaps, but an interesting challenge and a worthy part of your job description. It will probably help you to think of it as a game, as I always tried to do. It will definitely help if you can keep your sense of perspective—and your sense of humor.

Inside Meetings

Your boss asks you to set up a "simple" meeting for next week with the heads of all the departments in the company. Here's how setting up a typical meeting breaks down, step-by-step.

Step 1. Make sure you have all the details from your boss. How long does he think the meeting will last? Would he prefer morning or afternoon or does he want to hold the meeting over lunch? Should the guests be told the subject of the meeting? Will he be handing out an agenda in advance, or will the guests receive one at the meeting? Will he be needing any audiovisual equipment, such as an easel, a blackboard, an overhead projector and screen, a tape player, or a videocassette player? Will he want you to take notes?

Step 2. Check your boss's schedule to determine when he's free. Choose two dates and times for the meeting that are convenient for him.

Step 3. Call each guest's assistant or secretary and ask whether her boss is available at either of the two times—say, Monday at ten or Tuesday at three. Warn her to save both time slots (tell her to allow approximately an hour and a half or whatever your boss has told you the length of the meeting is likely to be) and tell her you'll get back to her.

Step 4. When you learn that at least one of the people can't make it at either time (in fact, one of the department heads is going to be busy all week), explain the situation to your boss and find out if the meeting is important enough to ask the manager to change his plans so that he can be present.

Step 5. Complete negotiations for the date and time and call each of the secretaries back.

Step 6. Send each assistant a note with the necessary particulars: where and when the meeting will be held, who will be there, what the purpose of the meeting is, and approximately how long it will take. Enclose the agenda if there is one.

Step 7. Deal with refreshments. If it's to be a breakfast meeting, find out what the guests like to eat and drink in the morning—

juice, coffee, tea, oatmeal, corn muffins, eggs Benedict, whatever—and order it. Arrange for someone to set up the buffet table or serve the food, whichever seems most appropriate. While you're at it, make arrangements for someone to clean up afterward.

Step 8. Order the audiovisual equipment and, if necessary, line up someone to operate it. Arrange for it to be taken away after the meeting.

Step 9. The day before the meeting confirm the time and place with your boss and then with all the secretaries. Make sure that your boss has the papers he needs for the meeting. If he has yet to dictate an agenda and you know he plans to distribute one, remind him about it.

Step 10. A half-hour before the meeting check to see that the room is set up the way you want it. If necessary, use a written checklist: the right number of chairs, an agenda for everyone, pencils, writing pads, water glasses, water pitchers, easel, markers, calculators, etc. Supervise the preparation of the refreshments. Finally, make sure that your boss's folder is complete and ready for him when he takes his place at the head of the table.

"Simple" meeting? The landing at Normandy was probably simpler!

Of course, scheduling meetings isn't always as complicated as the example I've described, but even if you end up skipping a step or two, your basic responsibility remains pretty much the same. When your boss calls a meeting, it's up to you to see that the guests show up on time with all the information they are supposed to have and that the meeting room is set up perfectly.

My Life as a Caterer

The only thing more complicated than setting up a meeting in the office is setting up a lunch or dinner meeting outside the office—at a club, a hotel, or a restaurant, for instance. That's when you end up adding Caterer, Protocol Officer, Stationer, and Florist to your job description. If you work at this job long enough, you'll probably become a real expert at picking locations, choosing menus, and arguing with waiters.

Some of the people I worked for liked to be involved in the decision-making process when we entertained outside; when that was the case, I found that the best strategy was to narrow any selection that had to be made down to three or perhaps four choices. Then I'd let him pick. When I was on my own, I'd start by asking the advice of the restaurateur, and then I'd solicit the opinion of a colleague or a friend who knows something about food and drink. Eventually I developed a list of restaurants and clubs where the people were most helpful and the occasion was most likely to run smoothly.

Relating to the Guests

I am always impressed when I see people doing a job well. I don't think I've ever been more impressed than I was with a receptionist I watched in action a couple of years ago. I was attending a good-sized meeting; about twenty of us were assembling one cold winter morning in an office in midtown Manhattan. As each guest arrived, she gave her name and her coat to the receptionist. A couple of hours later we trickled out, and without blinking an eye the receptionist handed each guest her coat.

I tried to let it go, but I couldn't help myself. When I got back to my own office, I called the receptionist and asked for her secret. "Nothing to it," she said. "When I take someone's coat, I just put one of those stickers on it with the person's name on it. Then I hang them up in alphabetical order. That way I don't have any trouble finding it when the person leaves."

I realize that the receptionist's accomplishment is a small thing, but as far as I'm concerned, these small things add up to a big, important aspect of an assistant's job. When you have visitors to your office, it's the small things that create the impression that you're a real professional—that you know what you're doing and you care. You're not expected to be perfect, but people have every right to expect you to try.

When your boss is hosting a meeting, it is your responsibility to assemble the guests, take their coats, usher them into the meeting room, and make them comfortable. If it seems appropriate, you might introduce guests to one another, but in most cases that chore is left to the executive. Once you are sure that the guests have everything they need, you may excuse yourself.

You need not feel compelled to get acquainted with the guests or make conversation, although one executive assistant I know never has much of a choice. Her boss, a high-ranking executive, never fails to introduce her to everyone who comes into the office. "I've been working for him for twenty years, and for some reason he thinks that everyone, from heads of state to the shoeshine boy, has to shake my hand and say hello to me before they can get down to business," she told me. She laughed as she described it, and I couldn't help but join her. I had never heard of anything quite like it. "Obviously it's not necessary, and once in a while I get embarrassed. But all in all, I have to say I enjoy it."

Whether you are introduced to visitors or not, there will be times when you will have to interact with them. This is especially true on those all-too-frequent occasions when the guests have assembled and your boss hasn't arrived yet. Your responsibility is to keep the guests informed ("He just called to say he's on his way. He should be here in ten minutes") and comfortable. If there is a delay, ask if there is anything you can do for the guest in the meantime. Would he like you to phone his assistant and tell her about the delay? Would he like the use of a phone himself? How about a cup of coffee or this morning's *Wall Street Journal?* Any kind of consideration along these lines makes a visitor feel cared for, which is always good but particularly desirable when he is being kept waiting.

Pride in your work should be enough to motivate you to be kind to visitors, but just in case it isn't, keep in mind another story I heard while I was gathering material for this book. One executive assistant so impressed one of her boss's callers with her skills and devotion to duty when her boss kept him waiting for an hour that he embarked on a crusade to hire her himself. She ended up making the move—and getting a 20 percent raise.

Every so often a visitor gets a little too presumptuous, or even obnoxious, and you have to put him in his place. That's what I did a few years ago when I worked for a CEO. As a meeting was breaking up, I was on the phone taking a message for my boss. Although he could plainly see that I was busy, a young lawyer stepped up to my desk and said, quite loudly, "I'll need a cab."

When I didn't even look up, I thought he would get the message, but no such luck. When I hung up the phone, he was still there.

"Didn't you hear me? I need a cab," he repeated.

"Excuse me?" I said, in my chilliest tones.

"What's the matter, can't you talk on the phone and listen at the same time?" he replied.

That did it. "Do you pay my salary?" I asked him, quite sweetly.

"No, of course not," he answered.

"Then get your own cab."

Now I don't recommend that you make a habit of telling off impertinent, ill-mannered visitors (I did so very rarely myself), but I must say it felt pretty good.

Interrupting a Meeting

Whenever there is a meeting going on in your boss's office, you should have a good idea how long he is likely to be holed up in there and if he wants to be interrupted for any reason. The better you understand your employer, the easier it will be to decide if and when to call him out of a meeting. When you do decide to interrupt, you simply knock, enter the room (you don't have to wait to hear "Come in" unless you've been told to do so), close the door behind you, and, drawing as little attention to yourself as possible, hand a note to your boss. He'll take it from there.

When a call comes for one of your guests, the decision making about whether to interrupt is out of your hands. For obvious reasons, it's not your job to decide whether or not someone other than your boss should be called out of a meeting. Make sure that the caller understands that you're going to have to get somebody out of a closed-door meeting. Then, if the caller asks you to, follow orders. Go get him.

Again, you knock, enter, close the door, and do one of several things. If you know the person for whom you have a message, simply hand the guest a note on which you have written the caller's name and wait for a reply. Sometimes he won't want to take the call and will jot down a message for you to give the caller. Most often he'll get up so that you can take him to a phone. If you're not absolutely positive about the guest's identity, let your boss guide you. Either say the name of the person out loud to your boss and let him point him out or hand your boss the note and let him pass it along to the appropriate person. In an ideal world an assistant would know the names of everyone attending every meeting in her boss's office, but here in the real world that doesn't always happen.

I've gone into a fair amount of detail about a straightforward and simple process because my experience has told me that an alarming number of assistants need this advice. Many is the time I have sat in a meeting with one of the executives I am working with only to have his assistant barge in and, leaving the door open so that all can hear, announce, for example, that Mr. Y from company Z is returning his call. At best this is a rude intrusion. At worst it is a breach of confidentiality. For all the assistant knows, Mr. Y could be my chief competitor. Even if that is not the case, it's certainly none of my business who is calling. And that goes double for guests who receive calls.

It is often necessary to interrupt a meeting in progress, but it is never necessary to be disruptive if you have good manners, exercise common sense, and exhibit consideration for others.

8

Travel

ONE of the most important parts of an executive assistant's job is maintaining control of business situations to the greatest extent possible. A good assistant will make every effort to anticipate her boss's needs and demands and plan for every eventuality, doing whatever is required to avert calamity. That's why no assistant in her right mind likes it when her boss goes on the road. "I don't even like it when he has a meeting outside the office," one assistant said to me. She was dead serious.

I'm sure many of you are thinking something like: "What do you mean? It must be *great* when the boss is away. At last, a chance to go to the dentist, get a haircut, or maybe even take a full hour for lunch for a change. It sounds like the next best thing to a vacation, especially since there are phones on the plane and everywhere else he's going, and we have the fax machine."

Well, yes and no. Yes, modern technology has made it easier to reach out and touch someone, and yes, once in a great while you get lucky, and your boss's absence does leave you with a little free time. But no, there's almost never a trip that goes without a hitch. Generally speaking, the time when the boss is traveling is about as bad as it gets.

Because you can no longer monitor your boss's activities, much less airline schedules, hotels, taxicabs, and the actions of all those with whom he'll come into contact when he's away, all bets are off. As hard as you try to make sure that an executive's business trip will go smoothly, there's always the distinct possibility that something will go wrong.

Making Arrangements

Coordinating travel plans is one of the most challenging and nerve-wracking parts of an assistant's job. Believe me when I say that you haven't lived until you have planned to the smallest detail a week-long trip to a part of the world you haven't even heard of, let alone visited yourself. If that doesn't seem hard enough, try revising a two-week itinerary because of an earthquake or getting your boss to a lecture three hours away in a blizzard.

Long before I had ever been to Europe, I felt as if I had spent months touring the countryside. I had committed to memory the names of hotels and restaurants in all the major cities, and there wasn't much I didn't know or couldn't find out about making it from one city to another in a hurry. Need a driver to take you from Florence to Venice? No problem. I even had the Venice water-taxi schedules for when you get there. I've still not been to the Orient, but I know their exchange rates, and if you wake me from a deep sleep, I can tell you what time it is in Tokyo and Peking. I also know the quickest way to get through customs and the direct numbers of the VIP service for every major airline.

Perhaps most important of all, I can tell you the fastest way to get just about anywhere. Experience has taught me that the most valuable gift you can give any executive who has to travel is time.

Like most executive assistants, I almost always worked with a travel agent when my boss had to make a trip. However, I learned early on (the hard way, I'm sorry to say) that travel agents can't always be counted on to get the details exactly right. For that matter, neither can airline booking agents or hotel registration clerks. After a travel agent gave me firm dates, times, and other miscellanea, I would always get on the phone, double-checking to make sure that no one had made a mistake along the way.

I would call the airline and have the ticket agent confirm every leg of my boss's journey, checking reservations, seat numbers, departure and landing times, and whatever special meal my boss wanted. I would also find out how long the layovers were (I tried to avoid layovers, of course, but that wasn't always possible). Then I would call the airport where he would have these layovers and find out about the facilities that were available there. Was there a VIP lounge? A health club? Were secretarial services available? How about a fax machine? If the airport didn't have much to offer in the way of amenities, I would try to find a nice nearby hotel where he could wait in comfort and perhaps do something productive.

If all this checking and double-checking makes me sound like a compulsive worrier, or even a nut, so be it. The truth is that I found that some sort of error had been made just about every time I made that follow-up call. His seat was next to the window instead of on the aisle, the low-cal meal he asked for hadn't been requested, he was in first class instead of business, or his wasn't even the most direct flight. Once I discovered that the flight the travel agent had booked no longer even existed.

I recommend that you double-check all travel arrangements, even if you've found what appears to be the world's best travel agent. It's a pain in the neck, I'll grant you, but it's a far sight better than picking up the phone and having your boss tell you that he's all dressed up with no place to go.

Preparing the Itinerary

An assistant I know whose diplomat boss travels at least two weeks out of every four, often overseas, spends a huge part of her time preparing his elaborate trip books, or briefing books, in which she describes in great detail every fact about her boss's forthcoming trip. In addition to the usual—flights, hotels, car numbers, significant phone numbers and fax numbers, pilots' and drivers' names, and a daily diary that accounts for every minute—she also gives him a thumbnail description of all the people he'll be meeting along the way. Naturally a man in his position can't afford to wing it or to make mistakes, so she spells everything out for him.

Even if your boss isn't even remotely connected to the diplomatic service, and even if he's spending three nights in Cleveland instead of three weeks in Moscow, you would be smart to take a page from her book. No matter how simple a business trip is, you should make it a point to prepare a written itinerary for your boss whenever he travels. (As I said in chapter 7, I used to prepare a kind of mini-itinerary for my bosses whenever they left the building!)

Don't leave anything out, including how he should spend his time waiting. I used to suggest that my boss call me at the office during airport layovers; sometimes we would spend as much as an hour answering correspondence over the phone. It often meant that I had to arrive early or stay late in the office or skip lunch, but it almost always proved to be time well spent for both of us.

One important itinerary item that is often overlooked is how long it will take to get from the airport to the final destination. Never assume that it's a short trip. It may be necessary to make the final leg of the journey by train or even helicopter.

When your boss is headed to exotic locales, it can be a challenge, to say the least, to get the information you need. Many people in the travel industry can be helpful, especially the airport chief of protocol, but I always found that my greatest ally when I needed to arrange for hotels, ground transportation, theater tickets, translators, escorts, and so on in foreign lands was the executive assistant on the other end. Certainly she is the most likely to be sympathetic to my cause. Many is the time I have booked a hotel room or made a restaurant reservation for someone who was visiting my town, and most assistants have been kind enough to do the same for me.

Arranging Air Travel

Once in a great while someone I worked for used a car or a train to get from point A to point B, but by far the lion's share of everyone's traveling was done by air. In some of the jobs I held it got so I could make plane reservations in my sleep.

My office would have put some travel agents to shame; at one point I had two atlases, a dozen maps, a large globe, and my own *OAG*—the *Official Airline Guide*. I also had a Rolodex that included the phone numbers of every major airport around the world (and a few you've probably never heard of), the chiefs of protocol of the airlines, and even the phone numbers where I could reach the ground crews. I learned from bitter experience that if you need to delay a flight or get a message or a package to a passenger in an emergency, the folks in reservations can't do a thing for you. Usually it's the ground crew who can save the day. It took me a lot of years to put my "travel information bureau" together, and it was worth its weight in gold.

When you're booking flights, here are a few small—but very important—considerations to keep in mind.

Know where your boss likes to sit. People always have a preference, and they almost never change their minds. Ask your boss once whether he prefers aisle or window and make a note of it.

Know what he likes to eat. A few years ago airlines offered an extraordinary variety of special meals that were there for the ordering—low-cal, low-salt, vegetarian, fruit, fish, kosher, and a few more I can't remember. There are probably even more of them now. Know what the choices are and find out what your boss's pleasure is.

Get the ticket and the boarding pass in advance. It saves time, and it all but eliminates the possibility of a passenger's being bumped on account of overbooking.

Know your way around private planes. I've never worked for someone who had access to a company plane, but I know a few people who have, and I envy them. Imagine a situation in which the plane has to conform to your boss's schedule instead of the other way around. Imagine not having to deal with baggage checks and boarding passes and security guards. Imagine being able to have his mail forwarded through the pilot.

I haven't had those luxuries, but I have had opportunities to deal with private planes when my boss was a guest on one of them. Along the way I learned a few important facts. One, many private planes take off from private airports; make sure you find out for sure exactly where the hangar is. Two, many private planes look alike; in order to find the one you're looking for you have to know the tail number. And three, it never hurts to know the pilot's name, not to mention his favorite baseball team.

Don't forget helicopters. For short trips they're a veritable godsend. There were plenty of times when I saved my boss a few hours on the ground by putting him in a helicopter.

Booking the Right Hotel

If you've ever walked up to a hotel reservations desk and seen a blank stare come over the clerk's face when you announce that you have a reservation, you know how horrible that can feel. You probably also know that when you're traveling on business and have a hundred things on your mind, it feels even worse. That's why it's critical to do everything possible to make sure that it never happens to your boss.

The first step is to choose the right hotel. I've met a few executives who enjoy quaint little out-of-the-way places, but they usually live to regret staying in them when they're doing business. They may *like* four-poster beds and antiques and afternoon tea in front of a roaring fire (who wouldn't?), but what they *need* is fax machines, mailing services, secretarial help, 'round-the-clock room service, great phones (including a direct line and an answering machine if necessary), and a staff who can perform miracles if called upon to do so. The hotel has to be conveniently located too, either close to the airport or right near the office or conference center where the executive is going to be spending most of his time.

Many hotels specialize in catering to business travelers, and executives usually develop a strong loyalty to their favorites. After all, the more often they stay at a hotel, the better the service is likely to be when they get there. One of the most important resources an executive assistant can have is a list of favored hotels in most major cities.

Making the reservation comes next, and here's where I turn into a compulsive worrier again. After being assured that yes, there is a room for my boss, with all the conveniences he'll require, I always asked the clerk for a confirmation number (some hotels call it the reservation number) and requested written confirmation. Once in a while a reservations clerk would try to reassure me that it wasn't necessary—"Oh, we know Mr. X very well here. There won't be any problem"—but I wasn't having any of it. I insisted on going by the book. Then, a few days before he was scheduled to check in, I would call the hotel and confirm the reservation again, referring to it by number. It's not impossible to be greeted by that blank stare we all hate even if you have a confirmed reservation, but it's very unlikely.

When He Goes Abroad

Domestic travel can be a real headache, but compared to arranging a trip overseas it's a piece of cake. Here are a few problems specific to foreign travel and a few strategies that can help.

The language barrier. Most business can be conducted in English, but if that isn't the case where your boss is going and he's not

119

bilingual, arrange for a translator. Check the embassy, the consulate, and the executive assistant in the office where he'll be doing business for suggestions. If you have any doubts about this kind of long-distance arrangement for something that is so important, recommend to your boss that he hire a translator at home and take the person with him.

The time difference. You can't do much about jet lag, but you can keep from being confused about "his time" and "your time." I used to keep a clock set to "his time" when he was out of town.

Passports and visas. To avoid hassle, make it your business to know the status of your boss's passport at all times. Visas expire more often, of course, so there is no way around having to get them relatively frequently. Give yourself a break and avoid the last-minute rush. As soon as your boss announces a trip, find out what sort of official paperwork he will be needing to get there.

Currency. We live in the credit-card age, but there are times when only cash will do. Find out the currency and the exchange rates for wherever your boss is going and write the information on his itinerary. Before he leaves, make sure that he has enough pocket cash, in both American and foreign coin.

Contingency Planning

I know one assistant who was awakened at five o'clock in the morning in the middle of her boss's two-week trip. She knew it had to be him. "He and his wife were on vacation for two weeks, but for them a vacation was always about 80 percent business. Everywhere they went they combined business with pleasure. It had been a complicated trip to arrange, involving a couple of planes and then a boat trip in the Mediterranean. When the phone rang, I knew it was about to get even more complicated.

"To make a long story short, the captain of the boat they were on had changed course, and instead of being in Monte Carlo as planned, my boss was about to land in Nice. He needed a place to stay, dinner reservations, and a revised itinerary for the rest of the trip. I had been planning to treat myself to a nice lunch that day, but I guess I don't have to tell you that it didn't work out that way. I had a taco at my desk and made transatlantic phone calls."

As my friend told that story, she laughed, and it was clear that she was used to this sort of thing. Any assistant whose boss travels a great deal gets accustomed to early morning phone calls and taco lunches. Eventually you're ready for anything: flat tires, snowstorms, reservations that don't exist, and boat captains who change course. There are always at least two ways to get something done, and a top assistant has to know what they are, even at five o'clock in the morning.

Staying in Touch

Many years ago the man I worked for was one of the first American businessmen to go to China. It was a complicated trip to plan, but it was exciting, and I really enjoyed the challenge. I learned a lot in putting together the trip book he took with him.

No one I have ever worked for likes to waste time, but this particular boss was a fiercely hard worker. No matter how far he traveled or for how long, he always managed to track me down to take some dictation or set up a meeting or give me some other assignment. His determination to stay in touch with me had become something of a joke between us. This time, though, I figured I was in for a real rest. Communications between the United States and China were very limited, and there was no way he could call me from Beijing. I planned to get my files, not to mention my life, in order.

The morning he left for China, I drove to the airport with him.

As usual, I had taken everything off his desk and mine, and we went through the pieces of paper one at a time. He talked nonstop all the way, dictating memos and letters, giving instructions, and reminding me about what had to be done in his absence. As he boarded the plane, he was still talking. He knew it was going to be his last chance to communicate with me for a good long while. When I turned to leave, I said, "I'll talk to you in three weeks," and I couldn't help but give him a triumphant smile. I was already looking forward to the luxury of his being incommunicado.

About thirty-six hours later my phone rang, and the man on the other end identified himself as the pilot of the plane that had taken my boss to China. "Mr. X asked me to call you. I have a couple of pages of messages from him. Do you have a pencil?" he asked.

Yes, I had a pencil.

Going Along for the Ride

In the old days it was fairly common to see secretaries traveling with their employers, but today it's quite unusual. Very few of the executive assistants I know go on the road with their bosses, and in all my years in the job I almost never did. The few I've spoken to who do some business traveling with the boss have given me to understand that while it sounds glamorous, it's not all it's cracked up to be. I must say I'm not surprised.

One assistant who used to travel a lot but now avoids it when she can said, "Sure, it's great to go to wonderful places—I've gone with my boss to Paris, London, Rome, and Rio—but the truth is I never got to see much of anything because I was working all the time, mostly taking care of him. One night one of his clients took us out to a wonderful three-star French restaurant, and I ended up taking notes through the first course and dessert. All in all, I think I would just as soon have stayed home."

9
Playing Politics

IT doesn't take a genius or a Machiavellian wizard to know that being an executive's "right hand" can occasionally mean sitting in the political hot seat. On the one hand, it's advantageous for you to know as much as possible about what is going on in the office. On the other hand, you can't be a buddy, and you don't want to be a snitch. As the boss's confidante you're in a privileged position in the organizational structure. You're not a vice-president or a top executive, but you are a representative, even an extension, of someone who is. In your interactions with everyone on the staff, above and beneath you, your behavior must be beyond reproach.

As long as offices are peopled with human beings, there will be, to some degree or other, office politics—jockeying for position, fighting over turf, friendly rivalries, and maybe even a little backstabbing. Like it or not, that's the way the system works in the real world. I don't have much of a taste for the machinations of office politics, but I do think it's important to understand how an organization runs and figure out ways to make the system work best for you and your boss.

The Code of Silence

I talked about this subject in chapter 4, but it bears repeating here. Anyone who gossips has no business holding down an executive assistant job. When you work for a CEO or some other executive at a high level, you know far too much about the inner workings of the company to engage in idle chatter with other employees. It's fine to be cordial to your co-workers, but it's a good idea not to make close friends on the job, even if that proves to be something of a strain. If you get too chummy, sooner or later you are bound to be tempted to reveal information that should remain confidential. In the long run you're doing your conscience a favor by keeping your distance.

"When I first came here, I went to lunch with some of the other executive secretaries a few times," one assistant told me, "but we always ended up talking about what was happening in the office. The strain of thinking about what I could and couldn't talk about got to be so bad I couldn't enjoy my meal. I finally stopped going. To be honest, I miss having company sometimes, but I know that being a loner is the best way."

It's trite to say it's "lonely at the top," but it's also true. When you report directly to someone in the company's top spot, you're in a difficult position. You're bound to like some people in the office and dislike others—you're only human, after all—but you have to do everything possible not to let your personal feelings interfere with how you do your job. It's not always easy to be a professional, but it's smart.

Naturally, that doesn't mean that you can sit in your fancy office (or more probably outside *his* fancy office) and ignore your co-workers. On the contrary, you need other people to function effectively, particularly secretaries, mailroom employees, switchboard operators, and other office service personnel. It is in your best interests to be polite, respectful, and considerate to everyone with whom you come into contact, even if you're not actually asking the person to do you a favor at the moment. If you're rude, overbearing, or otherwise difficult, you'll just make things harder for yourself in the long run.

Understanding Your Role

Once when I worked for the CEO of a large corporation, I was asked to host a luncheon for the five top secretaries in the company so that my counterpart in London could meet everyone at once. I was delighted to do it, of course, and I asked my boss what he thought about my reserving one of the executive dining rooms. He said it was a wonderful idea, so I went ahead and made the arrangements. Little did I know that we were about to make history. Never before had a group of "secretaries" been served a meal in our company's executive dining room.

Judging from the reactions we got when the news of our forthcoming luncheon got out, you would have thought we were storming the Bastille. Several executives were quite outspoken in their feelings, a few going so far as to discuss their objections with my boss. He stood his ground and supported my plan, as I knew he would, and, much to the delight of the dining room staff, who seemed very happy to see democracy at work, we ended up having a lovely lunch in the dining room.

Still, victory had a bitter taste. I did not really appreciate the reminder that in the eyes of at least some members of management (who had always treated me with respect and even deference in the office), my colleagues and I weren't good enough to eat with them.

There are several lessons to be learned from that experience, one of which is that it's vital to work for a boss who will back you up. Another is that an executive assistant must never be beguiled into thinking that she's an independent entity in the company, that she has any real authority. Whatever authority and respect an assistant commands come to her indirectly, because she works for someone important. To be quite blunt, it's your boss's clout that gives you yours. If it weren't for him, no one would pay much attention to you at all.

I know this seems so obvious that it goes without saying, but not everyone has the sense to realize it. An assistant I spoke to about this subject told me about someone in her office, the assistant to the executive VP, who had recently had a rude awakening when she left the job to have a baby. She expected to keep in close touch with all of her old "friends" from the office, and she was quite hurt when none of them showed up for her baby shower.

"It was sad, really," the assistant said. "Everyone had always been so nice to her, and she honestly thought it was because they really liked her personally. She never thought that they were just being nice because of her boss. It was a big shock when she found out the truth. She just didn't know the score."

Another woman I spoke to did know the score, so she was able to keep a sense of humor when something similar happened to her. After serving for many years as assistant to the president (actually several presidents in succession) of a small nonprofit organization, she left her post to take a middle management job in the same firm. She's happy in her new position and not a bit sorry to have made the switch, but she has noticed one important difference in how she is regarded now that she's no longer reporting directly to the man in charge. "No one listens to me any more!" she said. "When I worked for the president, people used to hang on my every word." She was exaggerating, of course, but what she said had some grains of truth.

I don't want to make too much of this relatively minor matter, but I do want to encourage you to keep your "sense of power" in perspective and to bear in mind always that while the power you have can be considerable, it's strictly second-hand.

When People Use You

"Call me when he's in a good mood, will you?"

"Do you know where he's having lunch?"

"I've heard that the company is going public. Do you think that's true?"

"I need another day on that report. Can you stall him for me?"

"What do you think this memo means?"

"Who's he been talking to behind closed doors all morning?"

If you're an executive assistant, you'll hear all those questions and hundreds more like them before you're through, and you'll become the master of the noncommittal answer. (I wish I had a nickel for every time I said, "You know I can't tell you that" to somebody.) Being used by people on the job comes with the territory. Most of the time it's harmless enough, and it can be quite satisfying to help if and when you can. There's nothing wrong with running interference every now and again. Occasionally, however, it can get out of hand.

Perhaps I'm too suspicious, but I have to say that if somebody in the office was overly friendly to me when I was an assistant, I immediately smelled a rat. I knew it wouldn't be long until the other shoe dropped and the request for a favor or some preferred treatment was forthcoming. Some people were shameless in their efforts, plying me with flowers and candy and heaven knows what else.

Most of the time my suitors were looking for inside information, poking around my desk trying to get a look at my copy of his diary or a letter I was about to send out. Even the mighty aren't immune to the desire to snoop. I'll never forget the time a senior vice-president tried to sneak a peak at my telephone call sheet. He stood in front of my desk pretending to make conversation, but it was obvious to anyone who cared to look that he was trying to read my boss's calls upside down. I tried to block his view, but eventually he went so far as to pick it up off my desk.

127

Obviously he didn't know me very well. I reached out, gently took the call sheet from him, and turned it face down on my desk. When he asked me what the trouble was, I said, "I'm sorry, Mr. Y, but you'll have to get Mr. X's permission before you can see that. It's confidential."

When he tried to pull rank by insisting that he just needed to check something, I got even sterner and said, "Mr. Y, you must understand that you're putting my job in jeopardy here. It's part of my job to make sure that no one sees that sheet but me and Mr. X." He got the message.

Some people have the mistaken idea that everything they tell an assistant goes straight to the boss, and they may use you to plant information rather than acquire it. Again, efforts to do so are usually pretty transparent, and nine times out of ten the message they want to convey is so trivial or pointless that you wouldn't dream of bothering your boss with it. Most of the time the best way to handle this kind of situation is to listen politely and just ignore what you hear, but if you feel that you are being badly used, it's certainly within your right to tell the person so. Gently but firmly say, "If you want Mr. X to know that, I think you should tell him yourself. I don't think it's my place to talk about it." That should make the problem go away.

Occasionally you'll hear something that you think should be passed on to the boss. You have to use your judgment about how and when to have that conversation. Once when I knew that the secretaries in my company were disgruntled and I felt that the grievance was legitimate, I told my boss. I chose the right time and gave him my message as subtly as I knew how. Another time when I learned that one of the staff was in financial trouble because of medical bills, I interceded on her behalf. On very rare occasions I gingerly called his attention to a problem employee. I see these kinds of things as a legitimate part of an assistant's job.

What I don't think is legitimate is snooping or spying on the staff, and I doubt that I could ever bring myself to do it. Fortunately none of my bosses ever asked me to, but I've heard of many assistants who weren't that lucky. "I wouldn't rat on someone in my private life, so why should I do it at work?" is the simple way one assistant described her philosophy to me. And that's precisely what she told her boss.

The Abuse of Power

As I said earlier, any power that an executive assistant has is a result not of her own position in the company but of her boss's high-ranking job. Second-hand or not, however, that power can be considerable, and it can be misused. I've seen it happen many times—an executive assistant who becomes mad with power and uses her position to take advantage of people and otherwise treat them badly—and it's not a pretty sight. At times the kind of arrogance I'm talking about is a lot worse than unattractive; when you mistreat the wrong person, it can be downright hazardous to your job.

A veteran executive assistant told me that she and the rest of her boss's secretarial staff take the responsibilities of working for a CEO very seriously. So does her boss. "There are several secretarial people in the chairman's office," she said, "and every one of us is conscious of the fact that when people hear us, they think that they're listening to the boss, even if that's not true. My boss and I have discussed it.

"Let's face it, if I ask someone to do something, whether it's a senior vice-president or someone on the cleaning staff, that person is going to assume that it's the president of the company who is asking and act accordingly. Of course, that's often true, but sometimes it's not, and it would be wrong of me and the others to abuse the kind of power that gives us. None of us wants to take unfair advantage of people. We're very careful of what we say and how we say it."

There's nothing wrong with having clout, even a lot of it, in your organization. Being able to command respect and attention is one of the definite advantages of doing this job. It can even take some of the sting out of the hard work and long hours. But it's important to remember that this kind of clout is useful only insofar as it can make your boss's and your work run more smoothly and efficiently. If you use it for other purposes and let your attitude get out of hand, you can do some real damage to him and to yourself. Enjoy your power, sure, but use it wisely.

10

Crises and Other Special Occasions

I'M fully aware of the fact that an executive assistant job is not right for everyone, and over the years I've gotten used to hearing people describe the many drawbacks of the position: hard work, long hours, difficult bosses, and so on. Normally I let such comments go unchallenged. After all, the work is hard, the hours are long, and executives are difficult. There's really no point in arguing. However, there's one comment I hear now and then with which I always take issue: "The job is just not *creative* enough."

Not creative? This is one of the most creative jobs I know. If you spend any time at all talking to people who do the job, you'll know what I mean.

Exhibit A. An executive assistant (number one of two) whose boss was planning to compete in the Bermuda Race some years ago discovered two days before he was supposed to leave for his trip that he needed a document he didn't have. What's more, the only place this document could be obtained was in Philadelphia. The next morning at the crack of dawn she and a sheaf of her boss's official papers, including his power of attorney, took the train from

New York to Philadelphia. When the office building opened, she was the first person in line.

Necessary document in hand, she was back at her desk in New York by noon. All of this happened without her boss's knowledge, by the way. Her number-two secretary had covered for her, and the crisis was averted. "I could have sent someone else, I suppose," she said, "but I didn't dare. If he didn't have that document, he couldn't make the trip—it's as simple as that. It was my job to get it for him."

Exhibit B. Another executive assistant was holding down the fort one Friday afternoon in her Manhattan office while her boss was on his way to his son's wedding. The family was assembling for the rehearsal dinner that evening in upstate New York. Just as she was about to leave for the day, she got a call from the boss's nineteen-year-old daughter, who was making her way by car from college in New England and had had an accident.

The girl wasn't hurt, but she was rattled—and flat broke. The assistant's first job was to calm her down. Then she put the girl on hold while she made plane reservations and arranged for a car to pick her up at the airport and take her to the restaurant. She even worked it out so that she could pick up some spending money at the airport. Finally, the assistant promised the daughter that her party clothes would be waiting for her when she got to the restaurant. Her next call was to her boss and his wife to let them know what was happening.

Exhibit C. An executive assistant's boss, involved in an extremely important diplomatic mission, left for the airport one morning to fly to Brussels for a meeting. Unfortunately, his portfolio—without which his trip would be useless—stayed back in the office. When the assistant saw the portfolio on the corner of her boss's desk, about a half hour before his plane was scheduled to take off, she grabbed the phone, explained her problem to the airline's chief of protocol, and asked him to hold the plane until she could get there. The protocol officer was skeptical, but she kept talking ("I might have exaggerated the importance of the mission just a little," she confessed to me), and eventually she made him understand that her boss simply *had* to have the portfolio. He agreed to hold the plane for fifteen minutes but no more. She flew into a cab, encouraged her driver to break a few speed laws, and made it with four minutes to spare.

I could probably work my way through the alphabet with exhibits, each an excellent example of how creative an executive assistant has to be. Every assistant has stories to tell, about discovering misnumbered pages on a report that has to be distributed in a couple of hours, about planes that got snowed in, letters that got lost, and best-laid plans that went distinctly awry. And as every assistant will tell you, when anything goes wrong, it's *all her fault.*

Keeping Your Cool

Every successful executive assistant I've ever met says that she's terrific in a crisis.

"I don't let things throw me. In fact, I thrive on stress. It gets my adrenaline going" is the way one described it.

"When something goes wrong, no matter how big a deal it is, I get very calm. The louder anyone else gets, the quieter I get," another said.

"I'm really at my best when there's a crisis going on. I think I go into overdrive or something," a third told me.

"I found out how cool I could be one day when my boss and I were riding in a cab, and, all of a sudden, there was a gunshot behind us. The back window crumbled, the cab driver froze, and my boss's face went white. I just leaned forward, touched the driver on the shoulder, and calmly told him to move the cab. After that day I was sure I could deal with anything," said another.

As I said in chapter 2, if you are going to do this job well, you have to be able to take crises in stride. When there's a problem, others can freeze or freak out, but you can't, because you're in charge. You have to keep your head. Remember, if anything goes wrong, it's *all your fault.*

Keeping your cool is essential in difficult situations, but sometimes you also need nerve. That's something I learned years ago when my boss of only a couple of months asked me to arrange a luncheon he was hosting for the Secretary of State.

I had never set up an event for a Cabinet member before, and I spent a lot of time on the phone speaking to a friend in Washington who knew everything there is to know about protocol. Naturally the guest list had to be approved by the White House and then screened by the Secret Service. Then the invitations had to be impeccably prepared and the program designed and printed. Compared to the demands of the paperwork, choosing the menu was a snap, but I had to see to that as well.

Things went along quite smoothly, but still, at eleven o'clock on the morning of the lunch—a rainy one, I remember—I was folding freshly printed programs in the back of the cab on the way to the club where the lunch was being held. My last chore was to set out the place cards on the table; my boss had specifically requested horseshoe seating, and I had to make sure he got it.

I arrived at the club, dripping, only to be told that women were not allowed into the dining room we had reserved. I told the guard who I was and said that I wasn't going to eat there, thank you very much; I was just going to check out the room, distribute the programs, and arrange the seating. Then I would be on my way. He said he was sorry, but he couldn't allow me to go in there.

I had visions of a luncheon without place cards or programs and said to him, without missing a beat, "Then I suggest you turn your back and close your eyes, because I'm definitely going in there." Then I walked past him and did my job.

"Plan B"

A friend of mine once told me that watching me in action could be downright depressing. "You're incredibly organized, which is great," she said, "but you always act as if disaster is going to strike at any minute. Doesn't all that negativity get you down?"

I'm afraid my friend is right about my attitude, and I have my years as an executive assistant to thank for it. She's wrong about its getting me down, though. I don't think that my way of looking at the world is depressing; I think it's sensible, and I'm sure that anyone who has put in three months on the job will agree with me. To me the best way to avoid a catastrophe is by knowing exactly what you're going to do if and when you're faced with one. That takes discipline, energy, and a lot of common sense. It means training your mind to solve problems even before they arise.

It also involves the kind of worst-case-scenario thinking that depresses my friend. You have to get in the habit of asking yourself what the bad things are that can happen and what you'll do when imagination becomes reality. When he forgets his briefcase, when the driver calls in sick, when the projector breaks in the middle of a presentation, or when you're faced with a roomful of strangers waiting for a meeting and your boss is stuck in traffic, what are you going to do? It pays to have an ace or two up your sleeve.

One veteran assistant who agrees with me puts it perfectly: "No matter what happens, I know that there is always something that I can pull out of a hat. I call it my Plan B.

"I had to put Plan B into effect just yesterday. My boss was expecting a really important ninety-eight-page document that was being sent by fax machine from Canada, and about two pages into the transmission, our fax machine jammed. I tried to fix it, but nothing worked. I didn't dare tell my boss about it, since he absolutely *had* to see the document before lunch, and he has a tendency to get a little irritable in a crisis. I just took a deep breath and thought of Plan B. In this case it was an executive assistant I know who works five floors up from our office. I quickly called her, asked if we could 'borrow' her fax machine for a while, and gave the Canadian firm the new number. Then I headed for the elevator."

Where to Go for Help

An assistant has to take initiative and assume responsibility, but that doesn't mean she has to perform miracles single-handedly. Even if you're the best assistant in the world, you can't do it all alone. For instance, when I needed help organizing that Secretary of State luncheon, I called a colleague in the State Department for advice. When that assistant wanted to delay a plane a few paragraphs back, she had the phone number of the airline protocol officer at her fingertips. Chances are if she needed to reach her boss at night in an all but empty office building with the phones turned off, she could do that too, provided she remembered that buildings always have guards, and guards always have telephones.

I've said before that it's critically important for an executive assistant to have a cordial relationship with everyone in the organization where she works, but there are two people who stand head and shoulders above the others: the person who heads the mailroom and the person who runs the messenger service. I'm not exaggerating when I say that I couldn't have done my job effectively without them.

If you ask people for their help, you'll usually get it. I remember once when I was trying to juggle my boss's schedule so that he could attend two dinners in one evening. The way I figured it, he could have cocktails and soup in one place and be in time for the main course and dessert at the other. The timing was critical, so I needed some help.

I called the person in charge of scheduling Dinner #2 and asked her what time dinner would be starting. When she told me seven o'clock, I pushed a little harder. "I know the invitation says seven, but I really need to know what time they'll actually sit down for dinner. My boss will be coming from the airport [this wasn't true, I'm afraid], and I may have to schedule another flight for him." She was happy to give me the information I needed.

Then, once I knew the last possible moment my boss could

arrive at Dinner #2, I talked to the manager of Dinner #1 about helping me arrange a quick getaway. "I'm afraid that my boss will have to leave the dinner a little early, so he would very much appreciate being the last person on the dais, nearest the exit. He doesn't want to disrupt anything when he has to leave." She too was most accommodating.

In order to enlist the aid of others, you have to know where to go. Here are some of the resources no executive assistant should be without.

Phone Numbers

A well-stocked Rolodex is one of an assistant's greatest allies. To do this job well you have to know how to reach an enormous number of people—CEOs, messenger services, radio cars, all-night dry cleaners—without wasting a lot of time. Make sure that yours includes the numbers of all major airlines (including protocol officer, VIP manager, and ground crew), helicopter services, car services, hotels, travel agents, florists, and personal shoppers in a couple of good department stores. Collect the names and phone numbers of experts in whatever field you're likely to need them. For instance, if you do a lot of business with the Japanese, cultivate a source at the Japanese embassy. Remember that assistant to CEOs in other companies are wonderful sources of information. Maybe you can help one another.

Reference Books

Back when I was an executive assistant, I was always looking something up in one of the reference books I kept within easy reach. Of course, I had the usual books—a huge unabridged dictionary, a one-volume encyclopedia, a thesaurus, an atlas and world almanac, the White Pages and Yellow Pages, the Directory of Zip Codes, a few hotel and restaurant guidebooks, Strunk and

White's *Elements of Style, The Katharine Gibbs Handbook of Business English,* and the latest edition of *Who's Who in America.*

I also had several other books with titles that might spring less quickly to mind, such as the *Congressional Directory,* the *Official Airline Guide,* the *Airline Seating Guide,* Letitia Baldridge's *Complete Guide to Executive Manners,* Standard & Poor's *Register of Corporations,* the *Encyclopedia of Associations,* the *Who's Who Directory of Directors,* and the *Diplomatic List,* which is put out by the Government Printing Office and lists, among other things, the names, addresses, and secretaries' names of all ambassadors.

No doubt there are many other phone numbers and books that will help you do your job, but I suggest that you use this list to get started.

Too Much of a Good Thing

I don't want you to think that every crisis an executive assistant faces is averted smoothly and that it always has a happy ending. Once in a while initiative can backfire on a person.

On one occasion I remember well my boss was behind closed doors at six o'clock one evening. He was scheduled to attend a black-tie dinner that night, and as the clock ticked away, I began to worry that he wasn't going to have time to go home and change and get to the dinner on time. I decided to act. I phoned his driver and told him to go to my boss's nearby apartment, pick up his formal outfit, and come back to the office with it.

Fifteen minutes later my boss emerged from the meeting and said, "I'm going to take the car home to shower and change for the dinner. Have the car brought around front, will you, please?" Of course, I had to tell him that his driver was on the way to his place, and his clothes were about to take a little trip to the office. We synchronized watches and decided that he would be better off if he met his clothes at the club and changed there. He'd have to do without the shower. Then I called the doorman of his apartment building and asked him to have the driver call me so that I could give him the revised schedule.

Obviously what I should have done, when I began to worry, was ask my boss what he wanted to do about the scheduling crunch, but I got so caught up in putting Plan B into immediate effect, I didn't think it through.

I guess there is such a thing as being *too* creative.

11

For Executives Only

ONE day the CEO I worked for asked me to put in a call to Mr. Y at the State Department. "I don't need to talk to him," he told me. "In fact, I'd rather speak to Ms. Z, his assistant." He knew that there was nothing he couldn't trust my colleague to handle, and I think he felt the same way about me. My boss had learned the value of a good executive assistant.

In the work I do now I try to spread that word. Every day, when my colleagues at the Duncan Group and I walk into executives' offices and talk to them about what they're looking for in an employee, we try to make them understand that selecting an assistant is one of the most important parts of their job. We want them to realize, if they don't already, that there is a lot more to the job than typing and taking shorthand. A really good assistant can transform an executive's life.

We make it a policy to visit an executive's office before we undertake a search. We can learn a great deal by talking on the telephone, to be sure, but we can find out even more by having a look at the work environment for ourselves. Over the years we've seen it all, from impeccably neat offices with hardly a sound to be heard or a scrap of paper in sight to the noisiest, messiest, most chaotic spots you can imagine. Of course, we're not there for the purpose of passing judgment on the decor or the noise level of the executives we meet; we're there to collect data. Everything we see and hear helps us to find them the perfect assistant.

How to Find the Perfect Assistant

When we meet with executives, we ask a lot of questions, and we get a few surprises along the way. What always surprises me, for example, is how little many executives really know about what they need and want in an assistant. Some haven't given it much thought; others have thought about it, but they haven't been entirely honest with themselves; and then there are the ones who are in a rut, unable to see that what they really need is a change. It's our job to help them get at the truth.

Normally executives are happy to talk. Even the most reluctant ones, those who think, way down deep, that the interview is a waste of time, almost always enjoy the truth-seeking mission eventually. Many of the people we meet find themselves thinking and talking about these matters for the first time. It's not at all unusual to have what was scheduled to be a half-hour meeting turn into a two-hour session.

Here are some of the questions we ask our clients.

What is her title going to be? If it's *secretary* or *executive secretary,* think about changing it to *executive assistant* or *administrative assistant.* It will probably make the position more desirable and expand your options. You'll end up with a better assistant.

What kind of turnover have you had in the position? If you're having trouble holding on to assistants, maybe you should take a moment and think about why that is. Perhaps you need to change your ways. Or you could be describing the position incorrectly.

What is the job description? Be completely honest here. Think about your typical workday and envision the part your assistant plays in it. You may be surprised to learn that what you thought of as "a little light typing" keeps her chained to the word processor all day. Or you may realize that what you're really describing is two jobs, a number-one secretary to handle your meetings and deal with the outside world and a number-two person for typing and filing. Many executives find that the two-person office works beautifully and is well worth the additional expense.

Which skills do you consider essential for the job? Think carefully. Many executives who automatically say, "typing and steno," forget that they haven't dictated a letter since the advent of the Dictaphone. In addition to the essentials, such as an ability to use a word processor and handle a ten-line phone, for instance, are there other skills, such as writing, that would make an assistant especially valuable? Should she know something about the industry you're in? As long as you're dreaming, you may as well dream big.

How do you perceive the role that your assistant will play in your office? How will she relate to you and others? How involved will you want her to be in your affairs? Do you need a self-starter, or do you give a lot of orders? If you want an assistant just to type and answer the phone, that's one kind of person. If you need someone who can take initiative and make decisions, to whom you'll be glad to give the run of your office (and possibly your life), you'll need someone with a lot more experience and expertise. Take some time to think about how much better your life would be if you could turn over more responsibility to your assistant. Maybe it's time to let go.

What kinds of personal tasks will your assistant be required to do? Again, be honest. It may be a little embarrassing to reel off a list of a dozen items, including "do my banking" and "pick out gifts for my wife" and "bring me coffee eight times a day," but you may as well come clean. She'll find out soon enough.

What kinds of things are most important to you? Are you a stickler for neatness? Maybe a phone that rings more than once drives you crazy. Or perhaps you're a fanatic about promptness. The person you're about to hire should know what you care about.

Are there personality traits you find especially appealing or unappealing? How important is your assistant's temperament? For example, are you the communicative type, or do you like things quiet? Do you like to chat with your assistant, or do you think she should be seen and not heard? Some secretaries need feedback more than others. Many executives find it helpful to hire someone whose own strengths and weaknesses offset theirs.

What is your office like, squalid and disorganized or neat as a pin? Some assistants thrive on chaos; others need an environment that is much more controlled.

How much do you travel? How do you see her role when you're away?

Are you a "morning person" or an "evening person"? Some executives hit the ground running in the morning and fade at four. Others are slow starters and get a burst of energy at three in the afternoon. Still others are high-energy all the way. If you want a productive office, you and your assistant should be compatible.

What's the bad news about your assistant's job? What problems is she likely to face?

What happens when someone who works for you makes a mistake? Think carefully before you answer; you may learn something. If you have a short fuse, you may as well acknowledge it.

When we ask these questions of the executives we interview, we encourage them to be candid and realistic about their needs. We often find that people have a somewhat distorted view of what they really need and want in an employee. One man started off by saying that he was looking for a really bright executive secretary, but it became clear that what would really make his life better was an assistant who could sit in on meetings with him and help him prepare reports, someone with whom he could discuss important decisions. We ended up finding him someone with an MBA. We've also talked to people who insisted that they needed someone with superior communications skills, a real "people person," when in reality the person spent most of her day transcribing tapes.

It's critical to find the right person for the job. An overqualified person will almost never work out—she can't help but be dissatisfied—but a slightly underqualified person who is eager to learn and grow can be the perfect employee. A B assistant can fill an A job, but an $A+$ assistant won't last in a $B+$ job.

Once in a while when we ask an executive a question, we can practically see the light bulb go on over his head. Obviously it had not ever occurred to him before that there was someone in the world who would do whatever it was we inquired about. "You mean I could really get someone who would be able to do all *that?*" they ask in amazement.

Yes, we explain. All you have to do is ask, and be prepared to pay the right salary.

How to Be a Perfect Boss

When I was gathering material for this book, I spent time interviewing many executive assistants, some of whom are relatively new at the job and many of whom are what I would consider veterans. One of the questions I asked all of them before we were through was, "If you had the ear of a roomful of executives who were about to work with assistants for the first time, what advice would you give them about how to treat them?"

Everyone had a ready answer, of course, and I was interested to hear them all. What I found especially enlightening was the fact that not one of them voiced a complaint about the hard work or the long hours or the pay scale. What they talked about were some of the aspects of the job that are more difficult to measure. Here's the gist of what they told me.

Be respectful. An assistant wants to be treated with the respect her job deserves, especially by the person who is in the best position to know just how valuable she is. Show her as much respect as you show any of your peers.

Be polite. At the very least, greet your assistant in the morning and at night and say "please" and "thank you" once in a while. You'll be amazed what a difference a few kind words can make.

Communicate with her. Don't make her guess what you want. Tell her what it is. Keep her informed about what you're up to. Compliment her on a job well done. If criticism is in order, make sure you do it privately. Public reprimands are humiliating and abusive.

Don't flaunt your power. She knows that you're the boss, that you out-earn her and out-rank her. It is not necessary to make a point of it.

Always back her up. If you ask an assistant to make decisions and act on your behalf, you have to stand behind her and trust her word. Loyalty works both ways.

Encourage her to grow. Be a mentor to your assistant. Give her a chance to expand her duties and responsibilities. Be a teacher. Never condescend or make her feel that she is unimportant. You need her and depend on her; make sure she understands that.

Don't take advantage. Most assistants know that your private needs are part of the job, but they all draw the line somewhere. Know where the line is and don't ask her to cross it.

Don't compromise her integrity. If you're involved in some sort of behavior that is not quite aboveboard, leave her out of it. Being a confidential secretary doesn't mean being a partner in crime.

Do something nice once in a while. Most assistants say that National Secretaries' Day sets their teeth on edge—I always hated it myself—but that doesn't mean they don't like to feel appreciated. Some sort of tangible evidence of that appreciation, such as flowers, jewelry, souvenirs from your travels, tickets to the theater, the ballet, the opera, professional wrestling, or whatever, is always welcome. And don't forget what Clarence Darrow said: "I don't know anyone who can't be rewarded with money." A cash bonus is always in good taste.

"I'm too busy to buy her flowers or say 'please' all the time," you may be thinking. "I pay her a good salary. Isn't that enough?"

Yes, as a matter of fact, it may be enough; there are many assistants who can live without the amenities, who get along quite well being treated like a well-paid piece of office furniture. Even so, I suggest that you make that extra effort, if not for her sake than for yours. You show me an executive assistant who loves her job, and I'll show you an executive who loves his.

APPENDIX 1

Tests

As I said in an earlier chapter, when we screen candidates at the Duncan Group we ask them to take a series of tests. If you would like to see how you rate, give the following tests a try.

If you don't get a perfect score on every test (or even on *any* test), don't worry. I like good scores, but perfect scores worry me. To be honest, a serious overachiever may have some trouble with the service aspects of the executive assistant's job. Some of the best executive assistants I know would miss a few here and there. Test answers begin on page 173.

Spelling

I've seen some pretty atrocious spellers in my time. One young woman wrote asking for a job and misspelled "secretary." I can't count the number of times I've seen "liaison" spelled wrong on résumés. A top executive assistant has to be a good speller. On this test we look for a score of 35 out of 40.

DIRECTIONS: Each line contains three spellings of the same word and the term *none*. In some lines, one of the words is spelled correctly. In others, none of the spellings is correct. If one of the spellings is correct, mark the corresponding letter in the right-hand column. If none is spelled correctly, mark a *D* in the right-hand column. You have five minutes to complete this task.

SAMPLE:

A. Conservative   B. Conservitive   C. Consirvative   D. None   A

---

1. A. laison   B. liason   C. liaison   D. none ___ 1.

2. A. anullment   B. annulment   C. annullment   D. none ___ 2.

3. A. attornies   B. attorneys   C. attornees   D. none ___ 3.

4. A. bankrupcy   B. bankruptcy   C. bankruptcey   D. none ___ 4.

5. A. counselor   B. counslor   C. counseler   D. none ___ 5.

6. A. cronological   B. chronilogical   C. chronological   D. none ___ 6.

7. A. cataclysm   B. catacylsm   C. cateclysm   D. none ___ 7.

8. A. exagerate   B. exagerrate   C. exaggerate   D. none ___ 8.

9. A. flexable   B. flexible   C. flexibal   D. none ___ 9.

10.	A. fraudalent	B. fraudulent	C. fraudulant	D. none ___ 10.
11.	A. hysterrical	B. histerical	C. hysterical	D. none ___ 11.
12.	A. infallible	B. infallable	C. infalible	D. none ___ 12.
13.	A. knowlege	B. knoledge	C. knowledge	D. none ___ 13.
14.	A. labratory	B. labortory	C. laboratory	D. none ___ 14.
15.	A. executrices	B. executreces	C. execitrices	D. none ___ 15.
16.	A. embarrassed	B. emberrassed	C. embarassed	D. none ___ 16.
17.	A. accommodate	B. accomodate	C. acommodate	D. none ___ 17.
18.	A. obsene	B. obscene	C. obcene	D. none ___ 18.
19.	A. occurrence	B. occurence	C. ocurrence	D. none ___ 19.
20.	A. offerred	B. oferred	C. offered	D. none ___ 20.
21.	A. paralel	B. parallel	C. parrallel	D. none ___ 21.
22.	A. perogative	B. perogitive	C. perrogative	D. none ___ 22.
23.	A. plagiarism	B. plagarism	C. plaigarism	D. none ___ 23.
24.	A. portrail	B. portrayol	C. portrayal	D. none ___ 24.
25.	A. priviledge	B. privilege	C. privilidge	D. none ___ 25.
26.	A. filial	B. fillial	C. filiale	D. none ___ 26.
27.	A. questionaire	B. questionnaire	C. questionnare	D. none ___ 27.
28.	A. recieved	B. receved	C. received	D. none ___ 28.
29.	A. repitition	B. repetition	C. repettition	D. none ___ 29.
30.	A. seismic	B. sisemic	C. siesmic	D. none ___ 30.
31.	A. sacrilege	B. sacriledge	C. sacrelege	D. none ___ 31.
32.	A. fluorescent	B. fluorescent	C. fluorecent	D. none ___ 32.

33. A. troglodyte   B. troglodite   C. troglidyte   D. none ___ 33.

34. A. separrate   B. seperate   C. separate   D. none ___ 34.

35. A. prefference   B. preferance   C. preferrence   D. none ___ 35.

36. A. recalcitrant   B. recalcatrant   C. recalcitrent   D. none ___ 36.

37. A. martryed   B. martyrad   C. martyred   D. none ___ 37.

38. A. paradegm   B. paradigm   C. parodigm   D. none ___ 38.

39. A. affable   B. affible   C. affeble   D. none ___ 39.

40. A. pecuniary   B. peciniary   C. peceniary   D. none ___ 40.

Grammar

My daughter studied grammar in the sixth grade, and as far as I can tell, that's the last she'll ever hear about it. I'm sure she's not alone. It's no wonder people do so badly on this test; a score of 22 out of 36 is not unheard of. We're very happy with a 30.

DIRECTIONS: Each of the following sentences includes two words, one preceded by the letter *A* and one preceded by the letter *B*. In the blank space provided at the right, mark the letter that precedes the word that would make the sentence grammatically correct. You have five minutes to complete this task.

SAMPLE:

Many persons were (A. affected, B. effected) by the transit strike.   __A__

---

1. Both Mr. Higgins and (A. she, B. her) were at the trial.   ___ 1.

2. Please get this information as (A. quick, B. quickly) as   ___ 2.
   possible.

3. Everyone has (A. their, B. his) own briefing materials of   ___ 3.
   the meeting.

4. Whenever he looks (A. sad, B. sadly) you can be sure   ___ 4.
   something is wrong.

5. Neither of them (A. approve, B. approves) the new   ___ 5.
   contract.

6. The company requires the form to be submitted by all of   ___ 6.
   (A. it's, B. its) employees.

7. (A. Whoever, B. Whomever) handled the case did a   ___ 7.
   wonderful job.

8. Either John or Mary (A. has, B. have) the directory. ___ 8.

9. Tuesday is (A. ladie's, B. ladies') night. ___ 9.

10. Both Mr. Carter and Mr. Smith (A. is, B. are) delegates. ___ 10.

11. He (A. set, B. sat) in the chair. ___ 11.

12. The hostesses will be two judges, Mrs. Jones and (A. I, B. me). ___ 12.

13. The article he wrote is (A. a, B. an) history of the event. ___ 13.

14. She could (A. of, B. have) gone. ___ 14.

15. Miss Smith, Miss Brown or Ms. Carter (A. is, B. are) here. ___ 15.

16. I saw in the newspaper (A. where, B. that) prices are rising all over. ___ 16.

17. The flower smells (A. sweet, B. sweetly). ___ 17.

18. She (A. use, B. used) to live in the country. ___ 18.

19. He (A. doesn't, B. don't) care; 20. he has already (A. ate, B. eaten) dinner. ___ 19. ___ 20.

21. Everyone in the group is concerned about (A. his, B. their) appearance. ___ 21.

22. He is (A. already, B. all ready) to go. ___ 22.

23. Is the hat (A. her's, B. hers)? ___ 23.

24. John asked if (A. they're, B. their) coming. ___ 24.

25. The noise of the engines (A. annoy, B. annoys) all the people there. ___ 25.

26. The doctor insists that the president (A. remain, B. remains) in bed. ___ 26.

27. Our greatest asset (A. is, B. are) our employees.   __ 27.

28. Try (A. and, B. to) be there.   __ 28.

29. They (A. saw, B. seen) to it that she got home safely.   __ 29.

30. Let's (A. don't, B. not) stay.   __ 30.

31. It is (A. everyone's, B. everyones') responsibility   __ 31.   __ 32.
to know that 32. he is the (A. principal,
B. principle) of the school.

33. The employee was granted a (A. year's, B. years) leave   __ 33.
of absence.

34. He has given us a quotation (A. on, B. in) which you   __ 34.
can rely.

35. Were you disappointed (A. with, B. in) the verdict?   __ 35.

36. All board (A. members, B. members', C. member's) and   __ 36.
their wives will participate in the weekend activities.

Vocabulary

This is somewhat less important than spelling and grammar, but we do look for a decent vocabulary in the people we place. A score of 35 out of 40 is acceptable.

DIRECTIONS: In the space provided at the right, please mark the letter of the word that means the same or about the same as the first word. You have five minutes to complete this task.

SAMPLE:

sensitive	A. delicate	B. easy	C. light	D. wavy	<u>A</u>

1. imbroglio	A. combustion	B. protection	C. confusion	D. formation	__ 1.
2. administer	A. manage	B. try	C. preach	D. disturb	__ 2.
3. admonition	A. connection	B. deleted	C. call	D. warning	__ 3.
4. congeal	A. join	B. solidify	C. hamper	D. weaken	__ 4.
5. tenable	A. reasonable	B. adaptable	C. unable	D. payable	__ 5.
6. dire	A. threatening	B. contradict	C. essential	D. official	__ 6.
7. customer	A. helper	B. governor	C. relative	D. patron	__ 7.
8. defective	A. subnormal	B. huge	C. pliable	D. transparent	__ 8.
9. enumerated	A. drafted	B. opened	C. pressed	D. counted	__ 9.
10. egress	A. upgrade	B. begin	C. exit	D. express	__ 10.
11. ethics	A. lists	B. rewards	C. standards	D. collection	__ 11.
12. atonement	A. appreciate	B. reparation	C. impenitence	D. unrueful	__ 12.
13. fraud	A. trickery	B. tear	C. agony	D. delight	__ 13.
14. fundamental	A. smooth	B. backward	C. secondary	D. basic	__ 14.

15. grapple	A. wrestle	B. open	C. insert	D. mold	___ 15.
16. illusion	A. frame	B. mirage	C. utensil	D. bar	___ 16.
17. indict	A. predict	B. inept	C. charge	D. release	___ 17.
18. accede	A. deny	B. forget	C. agree	D. challenge	___ 18.
19. thwart	A. effective	B. exonerate	C. block	D. distinct	___ 19.
20. merit	A. decline	B. deserve	C. observe	D. loose	___ 20.
21. oxymoron	A. contradiction	B. imbecile	C. chemical	D. gaseous	___ 21.
22. muffled	A. cornered	B. suppressed	C. widened	D. verified	___ 22.
23. optimum	A. sticky	B. forceful	C. best	D. worried	___ 23.
24. ostensible	A. distended	B. apparent	C. unusual	D. voluntary	___ 24.
25. peremptory	A. decisive	B. annually	C. running	D. dangerous	___ 25.
26. pilfer	A. recruit	B. perish	C. steal	D. freeze	___ 26.
27. prohibit	A. forbid	B. disgust	C. regret	D. irritate	___ 27.
28. anathema	A. command	B. distillation	C. curse	D. cleanser	___ 28.
29. distinction	A. distract	B. hasten	C. difference	D. obscure	___ 29.
30. stifle	A. prop	B. discourage	C. gun	D. twist	___ 30.
31. succinct	A. selling	B. sinful	C. concise	D. dreadful	___ 31.
32. sequester	A. isolate	B. aggregate	C. serenade	D. bequest	___ 32.
33. torrent	A. flood	B. machine	C. cord	D. tragedy	___ 33.
34. trespass	A. violate	B. mock	C. weaken	D. coax	___ 34.
35. dexterous	A. clockwise	B. happy	C. notable	D. adroit	___ 35.
36. utensil	A. board	B. implement	C. light	D. shirt	___ 36.
37. vacuum	A. soft	B. porcelain	C. gauge	D. void	___ 37.
38. verify	A. justify	B. confirm	C. destroy	D. imply	___ 38.
39. ossify	A. boycott	B. harden	C. sympathize	D. legalize	___ 39.
40. warrant	A. authorization	B. wreath	C. lawyer	D. convict	___ 40.

Proofreading

This test is complicated to score, since there are twenty-three absolute errors and a few "optional" errors for which you can be given credit. We look for a score of 18.

DIRECTIONS: Assume that a typist has just completed typing the copy beginning below. You are assigned to proofread the copy and mark any corrections necessary on the copy itself before returning it to the typist. Mark the copy in any fashion that clearly indicates the problems found and the corrections required. Standard proofreading symbols are preferred but are not required. Mark corrections only where necessary, *not* where you think it might make the copy read smoother. The emphasis of this task is to find errors in typing, not style. Pay particular attention to (1) consistency in format, (2) typographical errors, and (3) punctuation. You have five minutes to complete this task.

SAMPLE:

If shefor any, reason shall fail to qualify or cease to act as Executrix, I nominate Roberta coyle of 7934 69 avenue, Creede, Colorado 90404 as executrix.

If shefor any reason shall fail to qualify or cease to act as Executrix, I nominate Roberta Coyle of 7934 69 Avenue, Creede, Colorado 90404 as Executrix.

EMPLOYMENT AGREEMENT

Initial Term

1.   Johnson Corpration agrees to employ Hershel Jones, hereinafter referred to as Jones or as General Manager, and Jones agrees to

serve as General Manager of the Corporation for a period of 5 years
beginning April 1, 1983 & ending at the close of business on
March 31,1988, hereinafter referred to asthe "initial term."
Jones agrees during the initial, term to devote his best efforts
and entire time and attention to the business and affairs of the
Corporation and to perform such duties consistent with said title
  as may be assigned to him from time-to-time by the Board of
Directors. His compensation during the initial term shall be
$50,000 per annum, payables in equal monthly installments Jones
agrees to serve as a Director of the Corporation or of any

subsidiary if elected to such posts without additional compen
sation. During the initial term, the Corporation, at the discretion of the Board of Directors, may increase the compnsation
payable to Mones under this paragraph without affecting the other
provisions of this agreement?

Supplemental Term

3.   If Jones is still in the employ of the Corporation on
March 31, 1988, the Corporation agrees to employ Jones as a
consultant for a further period of 5 years beginning
April 1, 1988, and ending at the close of business March 31,
1993, hereinafter referred to as the "supplemental term".
During such supplemental term, Jones agrees to make himself
available for such advisory services as the corporation may
reasonably request, The Corporation shall have first call on
his time: but the Corporation shall not unreasonably inter-

fere during such supplemental term with any of his other activities. His compensation during the supplemental term, shall be at the rate of $50,000 per annum, payable in equal monthly installments.

Death provision

2.   In the event of death or permanent physical incapacity rendering Jones unable to perform the services which he is obligated to render hereunder this agreement shall terminate, and his compensation shall end at the close of the calendar month inwhich his death or such incapacity occurs.

Decision-Making—
The In-Basket Analysis

As you'll read many times in this book before you're through, one of the marks of a good executive assistant is her ability to juggle many tasks and do more that one thing at a time. This test measures your ability to evaluate the importance of a series of tasks and determine the order in which they should be done. This is one of the most throught-provoking tests I've ever seen. I hope you'll give it a try.

Today's date is October 14th. It is now 8:45 A.M. You have just arrived at work.

You are the assistant to Mr. Burke. He is leaving for an extended trip at 10:00 A.M. today. You will not have any way of contacting him during his two-week absence. This morning, he is expected to be in his office only from 9:30 A.M. until 10:00 A.M.

Several items are in your In basket when you arrive in your office. Other events occur as noted. In what order would you handle them, and what disposition would you make of each? You have 15 minutes to decide.

	Order	Disposition

1. A letter from a local high school teacher asks if Mr. Burke would address an assembly for business students on the morning of November 1st. The teacher has written you because he met you at a recent parent-teacher meeting and he believes you can approach Mr. Burke on his behalf.

Order   Disposition

2. Mr. Burke's secretary is out ill. Mrs. Burke has called with an urgent message that he must call her before he leaves at 10:00 A.M. The switchboard operator has sent this message to your office.

3. Mr. Burke has left on your desk a six-month plan that he wants to go over with you at 9:30 A.M. It must be reviewed before you meet with him so you can make any suggestions for changes. It will take you at least 15 minutes to review.

4. On your desk are the proofs for an advertisement due to run tomorrow. You must approve and return them to the production department by 10:00 A.M. or they will miss the publishing deadline.

5. A buyer is waiting for you when you arrive. She is upset about the proofs (mentioned above) for the advertised merchandise and wants to discuss some changes that she considers necessary.

6. Your secretary calls at 8:50 A.M. to say that she is unable to come to work today. She suggests you get a temp through Allied Temporary Services, a company that has serviced your office before.

7. Your secretary has left ten letters for your signature. These should be proofread before you sign them. The mail is picked up at 10:00 A.M., and they must go out at that time. Since she is not in, you must fold them and insert them in the envelopes as well as sign them.

Order   Disposition

8. The president's office calls at 9:00 A.M. She wants you to report to her office as soon as possible.

9. Several calls are flashing on your telephone, indicating that other people are waiting to talk to you.

10. Several weeks ago, before you knew your boss was leaving on this date, you scheduled an interview with an applicant for a position in your department. The applicant is waiting when you arrive at work.

The Essay

As if all these tests weren't enough, before we set our candidates free, we ask them to write a short essay—four hundred words or so—on the subject of their choice. Some write about their pets, their hobbies, or how they spent their summer vacation. One wrote about how much she disliked taking tests. We're not picky about the subject matter; we look for clarity, a strong style, basic writing skills, and decent handwriting.

APPENDIX 2

Secretarial Organizations

The following national and international organizations can provide useful information about jobs, classes, publications, and other resources. They can also help you to locate and join groups of secretaries and executive assistants on a local level. Write or call to ask for further information.

Professional Secretaries International
301 E. Armour Blvd.
Kansas City, MO 64111-1299.
(816) 531-7010

National Association of Executive Secretaries
900 S. Washington St.
Ste. G-13
Falls Church, VA 22046
(703) 237-8616

National Association of Legal Secretaries
2250 E. 73 St.
Ste. 550
Tulsa, OK 74136
(918) 493-3540

National Association for Female Executives
127 W. 24 St.
New York, NY 10011
(212) 645-0770

The Association of Personal Assistants and Secretaries
14 Victoria Terr.
Royal Leamington Spa CV31 3AB
Warwickshire
England
09926-24844

American Society of Professional and Executive Women
1429 Walnut St.
Philadelphia, PA 19102
(215) 563-4415

APPENDIX 3

Test Answer Keys

In appendix 1 I showed you five of the tests we administer when we consider potential candidates. Here are the answer keys for those tests.

Spelling

1. A. laison   B. liason   C. liaison   D. none   **C** 1.

2. A. annulment   B. annulment   C. annullment   D. none   **B** 2.

3. A. attornies   B. attorneys   C. attornees   D. none   **B** 3.

4. A. bankrupcy   B. bankruptcy   C. bankruptcey   D. none   **B** 4.

5. A. counselor   B. counslor   C. counseler   D. none   **A** 5.

6. A. cronological   B. chronilogical   C. chronological   D. none   **C** 6.

7. A. cataclysm   B. catacylsm   C. cateclysm   D. none   **A** 7.

8. A. exagerate   B. exagerrate   C. exaggerate   D. none   **C** 8.

9. A. flexable   B. flexible   C. flexibal   D. none   **B** 9.

10. A. fraudalent   B. fraudulent   C. fraudulant   D. none   **B** 10.

11. A. hysterrical   B. histerical   C. hysterical   D. none   **C** 11.

12. A. infallible   B. infallable   C. infalible   D. none   **A** 12.

13. A. knowlege   B. knoledge   C. knowledge   D. none   **C** 13.

14. A. labratory   B. labortory   C. laboratory   D. none   **C** 14.

15. A. executrices   B. executreces   C. execitrices   D. none   **A** 15.

16. A. embarrassed   B. emberrassed   C. embarassed   D. none   **A** 16.

17. A. accommodate   B. accomodate   C. acommodate   D. none   **A** 17.

18. A. obsene   B. obscene   C. obcene   D. none   **B** 18.

19. A. occurrence   B. occurence   C. ocurrence   D. none   **A** 19.

20. A. offerred   B. oferred   C. offered   D. none   **C** 20.

21. A. paralel   B. parallel   C. parrallel   D. none   **B** 21.

22. A. perogative   B. perogitive   C. perrogative   D. none   **D** 22.

23. A. plagiarism   B. plagarism   C. plaigarism   D. none   **A** 23.

24. A. portrail   B. portrayol   C. portrayal   D. none   **C** 24.

25. A. priviledge   B. privilege   C. privilidge   D. none   **B** 25.

26. A. filial   B. fillial   C. filiale   D. none   **A** 26.

27. A. questionaire   B. questionnaire   C. questionnare   D. none   **B** 27.

28. A. recieved   B. receved   C. received   D. none   **C** 28.

29. A. repitition   B. repetition   C. repettition   D. none   **B** 29.

30. A. seismic   B. sisemic   C. siesmic   D. none   **A** 30.

31. A. sacrilege   B. sacriledge   C. sacrelege   D. none   **A** 31.

32. A. fluorescent   B. flourescent   C. fluorecent   D. none   **A** 32.

33. A. troglodyte   B. troglodite   C. troglidyte   D. none   **A** 33.

34. A. separrate   B. seperate   C. separate   D. none   **C** 34.

35. A. prefference   B. preferance   C. preferrence   D. none   **D** 35.

36. A. recalcitrant   B. recalcatrant   C. recalcitrent   D. none   **A** 36.

37. A. martryed   B. martyrad   C. martyred   D. none   **C** 37.

38. A. paradegm   B. paradigm   C. parodigm   D. none   **B** 38.

39. A. affable   B. affible   C. affeble   D. none   **A** 39.

40. A. pecuniary   B. peciniary   C. peceniary   D. none   **A** 40.

Grammar

1. Both Mr. Higgins and (A. she, B. her) were at the trial.   **A** 1.

2. Please get this information as (A. quick, B. quickly) as possible.   **B** 2.

3. Everyone has (A. their, B. his) own briefing materials of the meeting.   **B** 3.

4. Whenever he looks (A. sad, B. sadly) you can be sure something is wrong.   **A** 4.

5. Neither of them (A. approve, B. approves) the new contract.   **B** 5.

6. The company requires the form to be submitted by all of (A. it's, B. its) employees.   **B** 6.

7. (A. Whoever, B. Whomever) handled the case did a wonderful job.   **A** 7.

8. Either John or Mary (A. has, B. have) the directory.   **A** 8.

9. Tuesday is (A. ladie's, B. ladies') night.   **B** 9.

10. Both Mr. Carter and Mr. Smith (A. is, B. are) delegates.   **B** 10.

11. He (A. set, B. sat) in the chair.   **B** 11.

12. The hostesses will be two judges, Mrs. Jones and (A. I, B. me).   **A** 12.

13. The article he wrote is (A. a, B. an) history of the event.   **A** 13.

14. She could (A. of, B. have) gone.   **B** 14.

15. Miss Smith, Miss Brown or Ms. Carter (A. is, B. are) here.   **A** 15.

16. I saw in the newspaper (A. where, B. that) prices are rising all over.   **B** 16.

17. The flower smells (A. sweet, B. sweetly). **A** 17.

18. She (A. use, B. used) to live in the country. **B** 18.

19. He (A. doesn't, B. don't) care; 20. he has **A** 19. **B** 20.
    already (A. ate, B. eaten) dinner.

21. Everyone in the group is concerned about (A. his, B. **A** 21.
    their) appearance.

22. He is (A. already, B. all ready) to go. **B** 22.

23. Is the hat (A. her's, B. hers)? **B** 23.

24. John asked if (A. they're, B. their) coming. **A** 24.

25. The noise of the engines (A. annoy, B. annoys) all the **B** 25.
    people there.

26. The doctor insists that the president (A. remain, B. **A** 26.
    remains) in bed.

27. Our greatest asset (A. is, B. are) our employees. **A** 27.

28. Try (A. and, B. to) be there. **B** 28.

29. They (A. saw, B. seen) to it that she got home safely. **A** 29.

30. Let's (A. don't, B. not) stay. **B** 30.

31. It is (A. everyone's, B. everyones') responsibility **A** 31. **A** 32.
    to know that 32. he is the (A. principal,
    B. principle) of the school.

33. The employee was granted a (A. year's, B. years) leave **A** 33.
    of absence.

34. He has given us a quotation (A. on, B. in) which you **A** 34.
    can rely.

35. Were you disappointed (A. with, B. in) the verdict? **A** 35.

36. All board (A. members, B. members', C. member's) and **A** 36.
    their wives will participate in the weekend activities.

178

Test Answer Keys

Vocabulary

1. imbroglio   A. combustion   B. protection   C. confusion   D. formation   **C** 1.

2. administer   A. manage   B. try   C. preach   D. disturb   **A** 2.

3. admonition   A. connection   B. deleted   C. call   D. warning   **P** 3.

4. congeal   A. join   B. solidify   C. hamper   D. weaken   **B** 4.

5. tenable   A. reasonable   B. adaptable   C. unable   D. payable   **A** 5.

6. dire   A. threatening   B. contradict   C. essential   D. official   **A** 6.

7. customer   A. helper   B. governor   C. relative·   D. patron   **D** 7.

8. defective   A. subnormal   B. huge   C. pliable   D. transparent   **A** 8.

9. enumerated   A. drafted   B. opened   C. pressed   D. counted   **P** 9.

10. egress   A. upgrade   B. begin   C. exit   D. express   **C** 10.

11. ethics   A. lists   B. rewards   C. standards   D. collection   **C** 11.

12. atonement   A. appreciate   B. reparation   C. impenitence   D. unrueful   **B** 12.

13. fraud   A. trickery   B. tear   C. agony   D. delight   **A** 13.

14. fundamental   A. smooth   B. backward   C. secondary   D. basic   **D** 14.

15. grapple   A. wrestle   B. open   C. insert   D. mold   **A** 15.

16. illusion   A. frame   B. mirage   C. utensil   D. bar   **B** 16.

17. indict   A. predict   B. inept   C. charge   D. release   **C** 17.

18. accede   A. deny   B. forget   C. agree   D. challenge   **C** 18.

19. thwart   A. effective   B. exonerate   C. block   D. distinct   **C** 19.

20. merit   A. decline   B. deserve   C. observe   D. loose   **B** 20.

179

21. oxymoron	A. contradiction	B. imbecile	C. chemical	D. gaseous	**A** 21.
22. muffled	A. cornered	B. suppressed	C. widened	D. verified	**B** 22.
23. optimum	A. sticky	B. forceful	C. best	D. worried	**C** 23.
24. ostensible	A. distended	B. apparent	C. unusual	D. voluntary	**B** 24.
25. peremptory	A. decisive	B. annually	C. running	D. dangerous	**A** 25.
26. pilfer	A. recruit	B. perish	C. steal	D. freeze	**C** 26.
27. prohibit	A. forbid	B. disgust	C. regret	D. irritate	**A** 27.
28. anathema	A. command	B. distillation	C. curse	D. cleanser	**C** 28.
29. distinction	A. distract	B. hasten	C. difference	D. obscure	**C** 29.
30. stifle	A. prop	B. discourage	C. gun	D. twist	**B** 30.
31. succinct	A. selling	B. sinful	C. concise	D. dreadful	**C** 31.
32. sequester	A. isolate	B. aggregate	C. serenade	D. bequest	**A** 32.
33. torrent	A. flood	B. machine	C. cord	D. tragedy	**A** 33.
34. trespass	A. violate	B. mock	C. weaken	D. coax	**A** 34.
35. dexterous	A. clockwise	B. happy	C. notable	D. adroit	**D** 35.
36. utensil	A. board	B. implement	C. light	D. shirt	**B** 36.
37. vacuum	A. soft	B. porcelain	C. gauge	D. void	**D** 37.
38. verify	A. justify	B. confirm	C. destroy	D. imply	**B** 38.
39. ossify	A. boycott	B. harden	C. sympathize	D. legalize	**B** 39.
40. warrant	A. authorization	B. wreath	C. lawyer	D. convict	**A** 40.

Proofreading

To score the test, compare the test sheet with the answer sheet below. On the test sheet, draw a circle around every *correct* mark you made. Then add up the number of circled marks and record this number. Next, add up the number of marks you made that are not circled. These represent *incorrect* marks (or changes you should not have made). Subtract the number of incorrect marks from the number of correct marks to obtain the final score for this test.

EMPLOYMENT AGREEMENT

Initial Term

1. Johnson Corpration agrees to employ Hershel Jones, hereinafter referred to as Jones or as General Manager, and Jones agrees to serve as General Manager of the Corporation for a period of 5 years beginning April 1, 1983 & ending at the close of business on March 31,1988, hereinafter referred to as the "initial term." Jones agrees during the initial term to devote his best efforts and entire time and attention to the business and affairs of the Corporation and to perform such duties consistent with said title as may be assigned to him from time to time by the Board of Directors. His compensation during the initial term shall be $50,000 per annum, payable in equal monthly installments. Jones agrees to serve as a Director of the Corporation or of any

close up (

subsidiary if elected to such posts without additional compen= sation. During the initial term, the Corporation, at the discretion of the Board of Directors, may increase the compensation payable to Jones under this paragraph without affecting the other provisions of this agreement. *11.* *12.*

Supplemental Term

2 3 *13.* If Jones is still in the employ of the Corporation on March 31, 1988, the Corporation agrees to employ Jones as a consultant for a further period of 5 years beginning April 1, 1988, and ending at the close of business March 31, 1993, hereinafter referred to as the "supplemental term" *14.* During such supplemental term, Jones agrees to make himself available for such advisory services as the Corporation may *15.* reasonably request. The Corporation shall have first call on *16.* his time, but the Corporation shall not unreasonably inter- *17.* fere during such supplemental term with any of his other activities. His compensation during the supplemental term *18.* shall be at the rate of $50,000 per annum, payable in equal monthly installments.

Death Provision
19.

20. 3 2. *21.* In the event of death or permanent physical incapacity rendering Jones unable to perform the services which he is obligated to render hereunder, this agreement shall terminate, *22.* and his compensation shall end at the close of the calendar month in which his death or such incapacity occurs. *23.*

Decision Making—
The In-Basket Analysis Answers

Note: This is an interpretive test. The following "answers" offer one solution to the various problems. There are other possibilities.

Order

1. A letter from a local high school teacher . . .

   Know if he likes or dislikes this type of speech. If he likes them, check with him between 9:30 and 10:00; if he dislikes them, write a declination letter later.   10

2. Mr. Burke's secretary is out ill . . .

   Hand a message to him when he arrives at 9:30.   9

3. Mr. Burke has left on your desk a six-month plan . . .

   Start this by 9:10.   8

4. On your desk are the proofs . . .

   Quickly review them.   4

5. A buyer is waiting for you . . .

   Make the buyer satisfied—spend 5–10 minutes with him at 8:55.   5

6. Your secretary calls at 8:50 A.M. . . .

   Ask secretary to call a temp from home or have another secretary handle (8:50).   3

7. Your secretary has left ten letters . . .

   Glance over them and sign.   7

   (Alternatively, this may be done while handling phone calls [#2]).

8. The President's office calls at 9:00 A.M. . . .

   Handle the call at 9:00 and schedule for 10:00.   6

9. Several calls are flashing on your telephone . . .

   Address crucial issues; call other people back at a later time (8:45–8:50).   1

10. Several weeks ago . . .

    Explain problem and ask person to return at another time (8:50).   2

Index

Index

Index

Index

Index

Translators, 120
Travel, 113–22, 144
  air, 117–18
  contingency planning, 120–21
  going along, 122
  hotel bookings, 118–19
  making arrangements for, 114–15
  overseas, 119–20
  preparing itinerary, 115–16
  staying in touch during, 121–22
  by women executives, 64–65
Turnover, 142
Typing, 20

USA Today, 63

Variety, 8–9
Visas, 120
Visitors, relating to, 107–109
Vocabulary, 21
  test, 159–60
Voice
  quality of, 23
  telephone, 74

Walters, Barbara, 15
Want ads, 31–32
Women executives, working for, 63–65
Word processing, 20
Writing skills, 21, 95–96

About the Authors

Melba J. Duncan is president of the Duncan Group, Inc., a support staff search and consulting firm specializing in the recruitment of executive assistants, administrative assistants, and office administrators. For ten years she was assistant to Peter G. Peterson, chairman of the Blackstone Group, former chairman and chief executive officer of Lehman Brothers Kuhn Loeb, Inc., and former Secretary of Commerce. For eight years prior to that she was assistant to Sanford C. Bernstein, chairman and chief executive officer of Sanford C. Bernstein & Co., Inc., a New York Stock Exchange member firm, where she was elected corporate secretary and stockholder.

In 1988 Ms. Duncan received a Women of Vision Award from the National Organization for Women, an award honoring women entrepreneurs. She has appeared on the "Today" and "Straight Talk" television shows and was highlighted in a feature article as well as the "People to Watch" section of *Fortune* magazine. She serves on the boards of the North Carolina Outward Bound School, the School and Business Alliance of New York, and the Dropout Prevention Fund. Ms. Duncan is a member of the Women's Economic Round Table and the American Society of Professional and Executive Women. She is married to Max Rodriguez, a telecommunications consultant, and has a daughter, Michelle. They live in the Park Slope section of Brooklyn, New York.

Kathleen Moloney is a freelance writer who has written or co-written books on a variety of subjects, including health, baseball, ventriloquism, and a book on etiquette for men, *Esquire Etiquette,* published by Collier Books in 1987. She lives in New York City.